100 Days to Freedom
from Shame

Copyright © 2022 Stephen Arterburn
Published by Aspire Press
An imprint of Tyndale House Ministries
Carol Stream, Illinois
www.hendricksonrose.com

ISBN: 987-1-62862-999-6

The views and opinions expressed in this book are those of the author(s) and do not necessarily express the views of Tyndale House Ministries or Aspire Press, nor is this book intended to be a substitute for mental health treatment or professional counseling. The information in this resource is intended as guidelines for healthy living. Please consult qualified medical, legal, pastoral, and psychological professionals regarding individual concerns.

Scripture quotations, unless otherwise indicated, are taken from the Holy Bible, New Living Translation®, NLT®. Copyright ©1996, 2004, 2015 by Tyndale House Foundation. Used by permission of Tyndale House Publishers, Carol Stream, Illinois 60188. All rights reserved.

Scripture quotations marked NIV®, are taken from the Holy Bible, New International Version®, NIV®. Copyright ©1973, 1978, 1984, 2011 by Biblica, Inc.™ Used by permission of Zondervan. All rights reserved worldwide. www.zondervan.com The "NIV" and "New International Version" are trademarks registered in the United States Patent and Trademark Office by Biblica, Inc.™

Scripture quotations are from the ESV® Bible (The Holy Bible, English Standard Version®), copyright © 2001 by Crossway, a publishing ministry of Good News Publishers. Used by permission. All rights reserved.

Written with Mark Atteberry

Cover design by Sergio Urquiza; layout design by Cristalle Kishi

Printed by APS
February 2022, 1st Printing

This book is given to

_____

on this day

_____

CONTENTS

Introduction

A person can feel many painful emotions, but few, if any, are worse than shame. To paraphrase the English poet Nicholas Rowe, shame is like having someone follow along behind you with a whip. No matter where you go or what you do, the pain never stops.

Yes, you can paste a smile on your face and pretend everything is fine, but you'll find that constantly faking it does nothing to make your shame go away—and eventually becomes its own source of pain.

You can try to dampen your pain by immersing yourself in worldly pleasures, but you'll discover that they have a short shelf life and always leave a bitter aftertaste. Or you can try to convince yourself that whatever you did that's causing your shame is a mirage, that you didn't really do anything wrong after all. But deep down you will know the truth.

The only real choice for overcoming shame is to humbly make your way to God, who invited you to cast all your cares and anxieties on him. That's what this book will help you do. Day by day, for 100 days, you will have something to read, think about, and pray over that will take you a step closer to God and to the guilt-free life you so desperately want and need.

But be forewarned. Because shame is tied to our weightier sins, some portions of this journey may be hard. There could be stretches that will lead uphill over rocky terrain. Don't let that scare you. Keep reminding yourself that what's *really* hard is continuing to live in shame. *That's* the outcome that is unacceptable. And, thankfully, unnecessary!

The Haunted Life

For I recognize my rebellion;
it haunts me day and night.

PSALM 51:3

Many cities, especially those that tend to attract tourists, offer "ghost tours." For a fee, you will be taken to numerous "haunted" or "spooky" places in the community and told about creepy or mysterious things that supposedly happened there. Nobody really takes the stories seriously. They're understood to be mostly urban legends or completely made up. This is the only instance in which the word "haunted" might have a little fun attached to it. Generally, it's a bad thing to be haunted, especially when you're the one being haunted.

The context of Psalm 51, which is our focus for the first week of this journey, is that King David was haunted by his affair with Bathsheba. And notice how he describes this experience. It wasn't that he occasionally thought about it and felt bad. Rather, it was something that ate at him "day and night." In bed, at the breakfast table, in a meeting with his staff, even as he worshiped God, he felt the relentless gnawing of guilt in his gut.

This sounds like an awful state to be in, and it is. But it's often the place a person has to reach in order to decide that enough is enough. As long as there's still some appetite left for pretending and denying and making excuses, nothing good can happen.

Are you being haunted by something in your past? Have you come to the place where you just can't take the gnawing in your gut anymore? If so, you have reason for optimism. You're right where David was when he began his comeback.

Any hurt is worth it that puts us on the path of peace.

Eugene H. Peterson

For Further Reflection

Romans 10:13; 2 Corinthians 7:10

TODAY'S PRAYER

Father, help me to see the pain I'm feeling as your megaphone. Help me to hear you calling to me through my pain, offering me a different life, a better life, a shame-free life.

The Bottom Line

Against you, and you alone have I sinned.

PSALM 51:4

Humans have an uncanny ability to complicate simple things. Perhaps you remember the Three Stooges clip of Curly trying to fix a leaky shower. He has pipes going every which way and completely traps himself. Helpless, he calls for Moe to come and set him free.

Something similar can happen to us when it comes to dealing with our sin. Our thoughts can chase down a dozen trails as we try to analyze our feelings and actions and the opinions of experts and friends, not to mention the circumstances of our lives that may have contributed to our choices. In no time, we're so confused we don't know what to think or do. Yes, underlying factors can contribute to our choices, but when we find ourselves living in shame, we are at odds with God first and foremost.

When David was feeling haunted by his sin, he reduced his situation to the simplest, most important truth of all—the bottom line: he had sinned against God, and nothing was going to get better until he faced that truth and did something about it. If you're living with shame, don't overthink your situation. You will have other things to deal with later, but right now this is between you and God.

Always remember that the bottom line is the starting line.

At the root of every spiritual struggle, there are two forces at war: not so much good and evil, but God and self.

Richard Exley

For Further Reflection

Philippians 1:10; 2 Corinthians 13:11

TODAY'S PRAYER

Heavenly Father, I acknowledge that I have sinned against you. Help me to always remember that I will never be truly right in any area of my life if I am not right with you.

Stop Explaining

Your judgment against me is just.

PSALM 51:4

There's an adage in politics: "If you're explaining, you're losing." The idea is that if you have done something that is sufficiently ill-advised that you have to keep explaining yourself, you're losing ground.

But explaining is what we do best, isn't it? I'm sure you've seen the T-shirt people wear around Christmas time that says, "Dear Santa, I can explain." In the Garden of Eden when God asked Adam if he had eaten of the forbidden fruit, he immediately began to explain: "Lord, the woman you gave me is the problem."

As David reflected on his sin with Bathsheba, he could have tried to explain:

- ∼ "Lord, I was so lonely."
- ∼ "Lord, I really just meant for us to talk a while."
- ∼ "Lord, she started it. Everything was fine until she started batting those eyelashes."

But he didn't go down that road. He simply said, "Your judgment against me is just."

I wonder if those were the words God liked best out of this entire 51st Psalm. They might have been, because they are, in essence, a statement of surrender. David was pleading guilty. He was choosing not to try and explain himself.

Have you been trying to explain away the sin that is causing your shame? If so, as the political adage says, you're losing. There will be no healing, restoration, or freedom from shame until you can stand before God and say, "Your judgment against me is just."

Most of us don't herd sheep anymore, but we keep plenty of scapegoats on hand.

David Jeremiah

For Further Reflection

1 John 1:8; Hebrews 4:13

TODAY'S PRAYER

Loving Father, help me to be honest with myself and, most of all, with you. When I feel tempted to explain, remind me that all I am doing is building a wall between myself and you.

Live Within the System

Oh, give me back my joy again;
you have broken me—now let me rejoice.

PSALM 51:8

David surprises us here with his choice of words. We know that it was his own lust that compelled him to send for Bathsheba, to sleep with her, to turn their one-night stand into an ongoing relationship, and to use his power to have her husband killed. Now, in the aftermath, with the misery of shame eating him up, we would expect him to say, "I wrecked my life. I did this to myself." Instead, he says to God, "You have broken me."

Sounds like he's taking a page out of Adam's book, doesn't it? "Lord, this woman you gave me enticed me to eat the fruit." The reason we know David is *not* blaming God for his brokenness is because that interpretation doesn't fit with anything else in the chapter. Again and again, David speaks of his own sins and of God's judgment against him being just. Clearly, he knows he messed up.

So why does he say that God is the one who broke him?

Because, in a sense, God did. It was God who established that there would be consequences attached to sin. It's like when a burglar breaks into a house with a security system and gets caught. Obviously, he has no one to blame but himself, but he could legitimately say to the homeowner, "You got me. The system you set up brought me down."

God has put a system in place that breaks people who don't respect it. But when we pursue God's righteous laws and follow his design, we discover great freedom, joy, and peace.

Sin is much more than breaking the rules. God created an intricate, interwoven cosmos, each part depending on the others, all governed by laws of order and harmony. Sin affects every part of that order and harmony—twisting, fracturing, distorting, and corrupting it.

Charles Colson

For Further Reflection

Matthew 6:33; 2 Corinthians 9:6

TODAY'S PRAYER

Lord, I acknowledge that there is something in me that wants to test boundaries and break rules. When those urges come, remind me that obedience is the better, safer, happier choice.

DAY 5

Amazing Grace

Forgive me for shedding blood, O God who saves;
then I will joyfully sing of your forgiveness.

PSALM 51:14

"Amazing Grace" is a song almost everyone knows, even people who never go to church. And they don't just know it; they love it. Try Googling "most popular hymns" and every list that comes up will include this song. But let's be honest—it's not popular because it's such a great piece of music. The melody and chords are so elementary that even a novice piano student can learn to play them. The reason it's so beloved is the lyrics.

Amazing Grace, how sweet the sound, that saved a wretch
like me

John Newton, who came to faith in his twenties, wrote the words out of the profound gratitude he felt when he came to understand that God's grace was bigger than his sins, which had involved everything from gambling to slave-trafficking.

Long before the song was penned, David experienced the amazing size and scope of God's grace. Notice, he asked God to forgive him for the "shedding of blood." King David was referring to his decision to send Bathsheba's husband, Uriah, into the heat of battle then have the rest of the troops pull back so he would likely be killed. David knew this amounted to murder, perhaps not in the letter of the law, but in the intent of his heart, because he arranged the situation, hoping to get rid of the man standing in the way of him marrying Bathsheba.

No matter what is causing your shame, you can have the same assurance King David and John Newton had: that no matter what you've done, even to the point of shedding blood, God's grace is big enough to handle it.

The parachute is strong, and the landing will be safe. His grace is sufficient.

Max Lucado

For Further Reflection

Ephesians 2:8; Hebrews 4:16

TODAY'S PRAYER

Heavenly Father, my sins are many.
Some would say they are too many to be
forgiven, that the stains they have left
are too deep to be cleansed.
Give me the faith to believe otherwise, trusting
your Word, which promises that your sacrifice
on my behalf covers my sins completely.

Broken Is Better

The sacrifice you desire is a broken spirit.

PSALM 51:17

We've all done it. We've all tried to make up for our mess-ups by making (or at least promising) some sort of grand sacrifice.

Take the husband whose wife looks at his phone and discovers some inappropriate text conversations with an attractive coworker. In his desperation to smooth things over, he will likely promise never to speak to her again, or any other woman for that matter. Or maybe a wife spends money that her husband had earmarked to pay the taxes. When he blows his top, she might promise never to go shopping with the girls again.

We are never more ready and willing to make a great sacrifice than when we have messed up and are feeling shame. But how many of those promises do we keep for more than a few days?

The good news in this verse is that God is not looking for you to purchase your release from the prison of shame with some sort of grand sacrifice. Promising to go live on a foreign mission field or give half your income to the church does not impress God one bit. What does impress him is a broken spirit. When your heart is broken over your sin—truly broken—he knows he has something to work with.

It took David about a year to become truly brokenhearted over his sin with Bathsheba, and even then, he wasn't truly contrite until he was confronted by the prophet Nathan. When that happened and his attitude changed, the way was finally clear for God to start working in his life.

Again and again, God's Word reveals that he is not as concerned about the depth or the extent of the sin we commit as he is about our attitude and response when we are confronted with our sin.

Nancy Leigh DeMoss

For Further Reflection

Psalm 34:18; Psalm 147:3

TODAY'S PRAYER

Dear Lord, in a world that exalts and rewards toughness, help me never to be so tough that my heart ceases to be tender. Remind me often that you value my tears more than my promises.

Bath Time

Wash me, and I will be whiter than snow.

PSALM 51:7

If you're in the soap-making business, you're probably piling up some serious money. According to Statista, over 1.8 billion units of soap products were sold in 2020. Body wash led the way with about 600 million units purchased, and liquid hand soap was a close second.

People like to be clean. I'm sure you've experienced that feeling of wanting nothing as much as you want a shower. Spiritual cleansing can be just as desirable. When you've done something bad and shame is sitting on you with its full force, the desire for cleansing is almost overwhelming.

In this verse, David makes an important point. He acknowledges that there is no cleansing like the cleansing God provides. We can do certain things to make ourselves feel a little cleaner, such as apologizing or making restitution or changing our bad habits. But what we really need is a deep spiritual cleansing, the kind that only God can give.

The good news is that he *will* give it. I particularly love the phrase "whiter than snow." What is whiter than snow? Nothing I know of. It's a picture of total cleansing, the absolute removal of every stain.

As kids, many of us hated bath time. Maybe you were one who ran and hid when you heard the bathwater running. Our mindset changes as we get older. The smudges and stains that our sins leave on us make bath time with God the most desirable thing in the world.

Parents are never surprised when their kids come in filthy from playing. Neither is God.

Anonymous

For Further Reflection

Psalm 51:10; Hebrews 10:22

TODAY'S PRAYER

Lord Jesus, I remember how you knelt and
washed the dirty feet of your disciples.
Thank you for showing us that you are not
put off by our filth, but ready and willing
to wash it all away.

DAY 8

The Power of Improvement

*Anyone who belongs to Christ
has become a new person.*

2 CORINTHIANS 5:17

Our verse for today is a powerful one, but one that is often misunderstood by those who are struggling to overcome a specific sin. It's referring to the cleansing we get when we accept Christ. God forgives our sins completely. Though they are as scarlet, he makes them as white as snow. (Isaiah 1:18) In my mind, this is one of the top ten most encouraging verses in the Bible.

But it suddenly becomes a discouraging verse if you misunderstand it.

Some people look at this verse and think it means that when a person accepts Christ, they are instantly set free from every weakness, that old temptations will no longer have their power, making life suddenly a piece of cake. Then, when that doesn't happen, they feel disillusioned and wonder what they did wrong. "I'm not a new person," they think, "I'm the same old miserable failure I was before."

If this is where you are right now, I have great news! The Christian life is not and has never been about sudden, overnight change where a person goes from deeply troubled to practically perfect in one giant leap. The Christian life is about daily improvement. "Growth" is a word the Bible uses to describe it (1 Peter 2:2).

And make no mistake, there is tremendous power in incremental improvement. For example, a baseball player who gets five hits every twenty at bats is a .250 hitter and considered mediocre. But a player who gets six hits every twenty at bats is a .300 and a star. That's just one more hit! The same holds true in life. Small improvements make a huge difference. So don't worry about being perfect, just do a little better today than you did yesterday.

When you're finished changing, you're finished.

Benjamin Franklin

For Further Reflection
2 Peter 1:5–8; Ephesians 4:15

TODAY'S PRAYER

Father, thank you for making my sins as white as snow. Please help me now as I begin to make changes to my habits and routines.

Yesterday Once More

*I—yes, I alone—will blot out your sins for my own
sake and will never think of them again.*

Isaiah 43:25

The Carpenters, a super-mellow 1970s pop group, had a hit song called "Yesterday Once More." The lyrics speak about hearing an old song on the radio and recalling pleasant memories and emotions that take you back to the good old days. People love this feeling so much that there are more than 400 oldies radio stations in the United States.

But what happens when the old days are not good? What happens when they are, in fact, the cause of your shame?

Those who are trying to overcome shame often encounter this problem. They hear a song on the radio, bump into someone at the supermarket, or see a Facebook post and suddenly the past comes rushing back. They've been trying to move on from what happened, but suddenly some random encounter triggers a memory and they're breaking out in a cold sweat and feeling sick about what happened all over again.

It would be nice to be able to anticipate those situations and avoid them, but we can't always. In fact, a better plan is to start fully embracing the truth that Isaiah shares in our verse for today, that when we humbly submit to God and repent, he blots out our sin and never thinks of it again.

The next time something triggers a painful, shameful memory, stop whatever you're doing and thank God for blotting out and forgetting your sin. Then ask him to help you let it go too.

We are products of our past, but we don't have to be prisoners of it.

Rick Warren

For Further Reflection

John 16:33; Revelation 21:4

TODAY'S PRAYER

Gracious heavenly Father, your promise
to blot out and never think of my sins
again is at the heart of my joy.
Help me remember your faithfulness
in doing this when the past threatens
to pull me back to unhealthy thoughts.

Facts Change

Anyone who belongs to Christ has become a new person.
The old life is gone; a new life has begun!

2 CORINTHIANS 5:17

Most people tend to think of facts as being unchangeable. For example, two plus two is four. The world is round. Water will freeze at 32°F.

While there are some facts that never change, we understand that many do.

- ~ 100 years ago, only 35% of homes had electricity.
- ~ 100 years ago, the Dow Jones Industrials Average was a whopping 62.
- ~ 100 years ago, a loaf of bread cost 7 cents.

If you're struggling to overcome shame, part of the challenge might be that you have not embraced a new set of facts. You close your eyes and see yourself as you were when you committed that terrible sin, without considering that God has done a work in your life and changed your heart and outlook. You are no longer the same person!

Our verse for today comes from the apostle Paul, and he's clearly zeroing in on this problem. He's impressing on those Corinthian believers (and on you and me) the importance of embracing a new set of facts. Whoever these people were in the past, whatever they did, however they may have blown it, they'd been made new because of what Jesus did when they accepted him.

This is the greatest news a person who is struggling with shame will ever hear. If you have accepted Christ's death on the cross as the payment for your sin and submitted your life to Christ, your facts have changed. You are not guilty; you are innocent. You are not dirty; you are clean. You are not lost; you are saved. It's time to start believing your new facts and living them!

Don't judge yourself by the past; you don't live there anymore.

Anonymous

For Further Reflection
Ezekiel 11:19; Isaiah 43:18–19

TODAY'S PRAYER

Lord, thank you for accepting me in my lost and broken condition and making me new. Help me to let go of the person I used to be and live as the new person you have made me.

Rude Awakenings

You will know the truth,
and the truth will set you free.

JOHN 8:32

Shirley Temple was one of the most famous child movie stars in history. From 1934 to 1938, she was Hollywood's number one box office draw even though she wasn't yet 10 years old. She once told the story of how, when she was six, her mother took her to sit on the knee of a department store Santa. The man playing Santa recognized her and promptly asked for her autograph. Shirley called it a rude awakening. She said she knew at that moment that something was off with the "guy in the red suit."

If you're struggling with shame, it could be that you've had a rude awakening, that some belief you once held has been shattered. Perhaps you believed you would always be strong enough to resist a certain temptation. Maybe you thought you were slick enough to keep some sinful behavior a secret from the people close to you. Perhaps you placed your trust in someone who turned out to be a con artist.

Whoever said the truth hurts wasn't joking. It often feels like a wrecking ball, crashing into our lives and laying waste to our cherished beliefs. But of all the pains we can suffer in life, this may be the most helpful. To finally be liberated from a lie and free to move forward in truth sets us up for greater success and happiness...even if it hurts at the time.

When you suffer a rude awakening, don't focus on the rude part; just thank God for the awakening.

The truth will set you free, but first it will make you miserable.

James A. Garfield

For Further Reflection

John 4:24; Psalm 145:18

TODAY'S PRAYER

Heavenly Father, thank you for always
telling me the truth, even when it hurts.
I pray that you will always put my welfare ahead
of my feelings in your dealings with me.

Do What You Know

*Remember, it is sin to know what you
ought to do and then not do it.*

JAMES 4:17

On any given day as you go about your business you can
encounter the following:

- ~ A motorcycle rider speeding down the road without
  a helmet.

- ~ Someone driving a car way too fast for conditions.

- ~ An employee or business owner who is rude.

- ~ A parent screaming at a child.

- ~ A person puffing on a cigarette.

What do these people have in common? They're all doing
something they know full well is either dangerous or
counterproductive.

You've probably heard it said that life is complicated. Maybe
you've said it yourself. And it's true to some extent. We
certainly do encounter tough choices along the way. But life
is not as hard as many people think. Most of the choices we
have to make in life are not really all that tough. One reason
is because we have the Word of God to teach us, along with
guidance from people who care about us, whether they be
parents, teachers, or mentors. Another reason is because we
have thousands of years of history to teach us what is smart
and what is foolish...what works and what doesn't.

If shame has come into your life, it's probably not because you found yourself in a situation where you simply didn't know right from wrong and made an unfortunate guess. What likely happened was you knew very well the right thing and simply chose not to do it. Let the pain you're feeling because of that choice teach you the importance of doing what you know is right from this day forward. It's not the things we don't know that destroy us, it's the things we do know but choose to ignore.

Do the right thing. It will gratify some people and astonish the rest.

Mark Twain

For Further Reflection

James 4:7; Romans 14:23

TODAY'S PRAYER

Lord, thank you for being generous with
your truth, for revealing everything I need
to know about how to live my life.
Help me to study and listen and learn,
but always to remember that simply *knowing*
what to do is not enough—I need to do it!

DAY 13

Not Even a Hint

*Among you there must not be even
a hint of sexual immorality.*

Ephesians 5:3 NIV

On the news not long ago, there was a report about a Florida woman who got up one morning and shuffled into her kitchen for her morning glass of orange juice. Disheveled and bleary-eyed from sleep, she almost stepped on the small alligator that sat in the middle of her kitchen floor. After driving it out of her house with a broom, she posted about her harrowing discovery on Facebook, prompting her friends to all ask the same question: How did it get in?

She confessed that the day before she had inadvertently left her sliding door open an inch or two. When she finally realized it and closed and locked the door, she had no idea that the little intruder had already gotten in.

This story is a perfect illustration of the truth behind Paul's statement in our verse for today. The "hint" of sin he's referring to isn't wild and reckless behavior. Rather, it's a mild flirtation with temptation, a little dabbling around the edges of disobedience. It's the equivalent of leaving one door open an inch or two. Nothing too outrageous. Nothing to be alarmed about. Except that a tiny opening is all an alligator needs to gain entry—and all Satan needs to gain a foothold.

One of the best ways to overcome shame in your life now— and to prevent it in the future—is to take purity seriously, to close up the small cracks in your morality. That means no toying with sin or playing around its edges. If there's even a hint of impropriety in what you're feeling tempted to do, don't do it.

Purity is always smart; impurity is always stupid. Not sometimes. Not usually. Always.

Randy Alcorn

For Further Reflection

Psalm 119:9; Matthew 5:8

TODAY'S PRAYER

Dear Father, help me to be more attentive to the details of my life. May I not be so focused on the big things Satan is doing that I fail to remember his love for small openings and opportunities.

Confession

If we confess our sins to him,
he is faithful and just to forgive us our sins
and to cleanse us from all wickedness.

1 JOHN 1:9

If you're being crushed under a load of shame right now, you'll no doubt be drawn to the words "forgive" and "cleanse" in this verse. You'll see them as the perfect antidote to your problem. They'll no doubt spark feelings of hope in your heart and prompt your pulse to quicken. But save those words for later—because first you must wrestle with the word "confess."

John says this wonderful forgiveness and cleansing hinges on our willingness to confess our sins. The first truth to note is that a confession is not an explanation. Perhaps you've noticed that celebrities and politicians who get caught in illicit behavior often make a statement to the press that is carefully crafted to explain what happened and put the best possible spin on it. This is not what John is talking about.

Second, a confession is not a strategy. Those who make their living doing damage control say that it's always best to get out in front of a scandal. The best strategy is to admit what you did before the press breaks the story. You always look worse if you're on defense than if you're on offense.

The confession John is referring to here is very raw and real. You don't explain and you don't spin. You lay your soul bare before the Lord and admit what you've done, period.

Resurrection is no effort for God. His only problem is to get us to lay down and admit that we are dead.

George Mallone

For Further Reflection

Proverbs 28:13; Psalm 32:5

TODAY'S PRAYER

Lord, I acknowledge that I have sinned.
Forgive me for those times I have tried
to spin my actions, shift blame, or try
to make myself look better than I am.
Help me to remember that the cleansing I long
for demands my honesty before you.

Incoming!

*Be careful not to fall into the
same temptation yourself.*

GALATIANS 6:1

When you've made a terrible mistake and are feeling shame, there's a lot of hard stuff to deal with. Something that is rarely discussed is the pain of judgment and criticism that is hurled at you, often by fellow brothers and sisters in Christ. In Matthew 7:1 Jesus told us not to judge others, but that doesn't slow most people down.

People *are* going to throw stones. You won't be able to stop this from happening. It's one of the many consequences of sin, and one we don't think about until it happens. The important thing for you is to resist the temptation to return fire.

If someone calls you a hypocrite, you might immediately recall a time when that person did something very hypocritical.

If someone speaks to you sarcastically, you could easily slip into sarcasm and fire a smart-aleck remark right back.

If someone gives you the cold shoulder, you might decide you're never going to have anything to do with that person again.

These are common, human responses, but they are extremely unhealthy. At a time when you're seeking healing and restoration, such tit-for-tat responses lock you into negative thoughts and feelings. You will be very wise to immediately forgive anyone who attacks you, for their sake, certainly, but mostly for your own. You desperately need cleansing—and getting into a shootout with your critics will lead you away from it, not toward it.

Be careful who you choose as your enemy because that's who you become most like.

Friedrich Nietzsche

For Further Reflection

Colossians 3:13; Proverbs 12:16

TODAY'S PRAYER

Father, remind me every day that your opinion of me matters more than anyone else's. Give me the strength to turn the other cheek when people attack me, and to forgive them the way you have forgiven me.

Religion Is Not the Answer

They crush people with unbearable religious demands.

MATHEW 23:4

I f you have committed a grievous sin and are suffering shame, it won't be long until some Christian will advise you to include more religious activities in your routine to heal and, of course, become a better person. You'll be told you need to join a small group, go to a retreat, find an accountability partner, pray more, read the Bible more, serve more, give more, and be more expressive when you worship. They may not say the actual words, but they're essentially telling you that your whole problem is that you aren't religious enough.

Be wary of these people. They mean well, but they fail to recognize a truth that Jesus called attention to throughout his ministry: Religion often makes us worse people, not better. The Pharisees, for example, were the religious superstars of their day, yet Jesus criticized them more than he did anybody else. Even more telling is the fact that Jesus was constantly criticized for not being religious enough, which was okay with him. He went to great lengths to separate himself from the religiosity of his day.

If you have committed sin and are suffering shame, what you need more than anything is to walk more closely with Jesus, which means the last thing you want to do is pursue the very thing he avoided. Think about it. If you're chasing what he avoided, how can you possibly be walking *with* him?

Forget the outer trappings of religion and just get close to Jesus. Read and ponder his words, observe his actions, follow his example, adopt his priorities, and be receptive to his Spirit. Such things will help you more than all religious activities in the world.

This is what makes religion so frustrating. It bases life on impossible standards, makes you feel guilty for missing them, and leaves you powerless to do anything about it.

Kyle Idleman

For Further Reflection

Micah 6:8; Romans 14:17

TODAY'S PRAYER

Lord Jesus, help me not to be deceived into believing religion is what I need. When others try to point me toward rules and rituals, remind me to keep my eyes and my heart squarely on you.

Who (or What) Is Your Enemy?

My enemies have set a trap for me.
I am weary from distress.

PSALM 57:6

There's an old joke about an overweight guy who was on a diet. He'd been trying really hard, so one day he decided to reward himself with a donut on his way to work. But then he wondered if God would approve. So he prayed, "Lord, if there's a parking space by the front door of the donut shop, I'll take it as a sign from you that you approve of me having a donut this morning." When he got to the donut shop, he was pleased that he only had to drive around the block nine times to find a parking space by the front door.

The Bible says that Satan is our enemy, and he is. But in this psalm, and others, David reminds us that we can have many enemies. Sometimes a donut can be your enemy. Or maybe a website that you can't seem to stay away from. Or a fear that keeps you from pursuing your dreams. Or a coworker who flirts with you even though one or both of you is married.

Enemies take many forms, but there's one thing they all have in common: They set traps for you, always in the area of your greatest weaknesses. These traps are effective, as evidenced by the number of people now facing the aftermath of sin and shame. Maybe they had their guard down, or maybe they didn't realize the object in question was so dangerous.

What is dangerous to you? If you're suffering chagrin over past failure, you likely already know at least one object, person, or temptation that qualifies as an enemy. Are there others? This is an important question as you move forward. Identifying your enemies will help you make sense of the past and make better choices in the future.

Death is not the enemy; snakes are. And cheese: it is addictive and irresistible. I have had three kinds so far today.

Anne Lamott

For Further Reflection

Proverbs 27:12; Proverbs 14:16

TODAY'S PRAYER

Father in heaven, give me eyes to see the people and things around me that are dangerous to my faith and obedience. And give me the strength to avoid them.

Life in a Fallen World

When Adam sinned, sin entered the world.

Romans 5:12

Have you ever had one of those "everything is different now" moments?

Maybe it was the first time you laid eyes on your future mate.

Maybe it was the moment you first learned you were going to become a parent.

Maybe it was the moment you realized that someone you trusted had betrayed you.

The greatest "everything is different now" moment in all of history happened in the Garden of Eden when Adam and Eve chose to disobey God and eat the forbidden fruit. Before that, everything was perfect. Afterward, not so much. Even though God warned them that tough times were ahead, Adam and Eve probably had little idea just how tough life would turn out to be. You can almost imagine them tilling the ground with the sting of sweat in their eyes and pain in their lower backs, thinking, "Boy, I wish we could have a do-over!"

But there were no do-overs, and so you and I are stuck living in a sinful, fallen world. What this means is that there are traps and snares everywhere. Just about anything you encounter can be dangerous, even things that God created and that are good. Sex and food are classic examples.

Chances are good that the reason you're dealing with shame right now is because you stepped into a trap. Maybe you didn't see it coming, or maybe you did and made a bad choice. Either way, more trouble is in your future if you don't start thinking more seriously about the kind of world you live in and what it takes to keep yourself right with God.

We can't afford to be careless. We don't live in a morally neutral environment. It's not safe out there.

Andy Stanley

For Further Reflection

Romans 5:12; Ephesians 6:11

TODAY'S PRAYER

Lord, give me wisdom, that I might recognize
the traps and snares I encounter.
Remind me often that this world is
neither my home nor my friend.

Daily

His mercies begin afresh each morning.

LAMENTATIONS 3:23

It's impossible to read the Bible without noticing that the life of faith is intended to be a daily proposition. In the wilderness, for example, the Israelites were promised manna, but not in weekly or monthly shipments. They were told it would come to them every day. When Jesus gave us the model prayer, he didn't ask for supplies to sock away for a rainy day; he simply asked for "daily bread." And in our verse for today, which is one of the most encouraging in the entire Bible, we're told that God's mercies begin fresh every morning.

People who are suffering from shame tend to think in increments of time that are far too large. Right now, you might be looking back and reflecting on the things you did that got you into trouble. Even though there's nothing you can do to change your choices, you may be allowing them to eat at you. Or you might be looking ahead, trying to imagine how your life will be different now that you've sinned so grievously. How will your actions affect your relationships, your reputation, or your future?

God would encourage you to release the past, quit worrying about the future, and just focus on one day at a time. You've probably seen promotional giveaways that stipulate, "You must be present to win." That's a good motto for our lives. You've got to be present—here, now, today—to gain the blessing God has prepared for you. Don't let the ghosts of yesterday or worries about tomorrow steal your blessing.

Doesn't every day deserve a chance to be a good day?

Max Lucado

For Further Reflection

Psalm 118:24; 2 Corinthians 4:16

TODAY'S PRAYER

Jesus, I feel the angst of yesterday and tomorrow pulling at me, trying to keep me from focusing on today. Give me the strength to resist the distractions and simply enjoy my time with you here and now.

Roots Matter

They are like trees planted along the riverbank,
bearing fruit each season.

PSALM 1:3

Have you noticed that landscapers use long pieces of wood to prop up newly planted trees? It looks terrible, doesn't it? All the perfectly positioned plants, neatly trimmed and surrounded by fresh mulch...ruined by those boards going every which way. But without that reinforcement, the trees would be in trouble. Unless their roots have a chance to sink deep into the ground, the first good storm that comes along will blow them down.

Is the reason you're struggling to overcome shame because you didn't have deep enough roots when a trial or temptation came along? You may have looked the part of a great Christian, just as a newly planted tree can be gorgeous. You may have attended church every week and even served in some key capacity. People may have admired you, wanted to be like you. But if you aren't deeply rooted in Christ, you're vulnerable, no matter how strong you appear.

In today's verse, the psalmist uses the metaphor of a tree planted by a riverbank to describe someone who is completely committed to God. Riverbank trees are healthy trees because of the water source and nutrients in the soil. The roots are fed well and sink deep into the ground, making the tree a tower of strength that is not easily toppled.

An important part of overcoming shame is growing stronger so you don't repeat your wrongdoing. We live in a world obsessed with appearance, but it's those unseen roots that are most important. It's what you're doing that people *can't* see—your inner spiritual walk with God and daily obedience to his will—that will determine how strongly you stand in the next storm.

There's no fruit without some kind of root.

Louie Giglio

For Further Reflection

Colossians 2:6–7; Mark 4:17

TODAY'S PRAYER

Dear Father, forgive me for being content with looking like a good Christian. Help me now to grow into one by sinking my spiritual roots down deep into you and your Word.

Good News / Bad News

Peter's words pierced their hearts,
and they said to him and the other apostles,
"Brothers, what should we do?"

ACTS 2:37

One day a man walked up to his friend and said, "I have good news and bad news." His friend said, "Look, I'm a positive guy. I'm not into negativity at all. So just give me the good news and forget the bad news." His friend said, "Okay, here's your car keys back. Thanks for letting me borrow your car. I'm happy to report that your air bags work perfectly."

Good news and bad news often go hand in hand.

In today's verse, Peter has just finished preaching arguably the most important sermon ever preached, the sermon that would result in 3,000 baptisms and launch the Church. And he finished with some really bad news. He told the Jews in his audience that they were guilty of killing Jesus, the Messiah. The people felt the sting of those words and asked if there was a way to get rid of their guilt. That's when Peter gave them the good news—that they could repent, turn to God, be baptized, and be saved.

Bad news, followed quickly by good news.

This is the Gospel in a nutshell.

Unfortunately, many people just want the good news part of the Gospel. They want to hear about Jesus' love and grace and mercy, but they'd prefer not to think about their sin. However, it's after we deal with our sin that we can truly appreciate the good news of forgiveness and salvation.

If you are reckoning with your sin right now—if you're feeling the pain, the regret, and the shame of it—that's a good thing. You don't want to live in that place forever, but for now that pain will help you appreciate what Jesus did for you.

The Gospel is bad news before it is good news.

Frederick Buechner

For Further Reflection

Hosea 6:1; 1 Thessalonians 5:18

TODAY'S PRAYER

Lord Jesus, thank you for dying on the cross to remove all my sin. You are not just Good News; you are the Best News. Help me to show my gratitude in the way I live from now on.

Tandem Sinning

*Let the one who has never sinned
throw the first stone.*

JOHN 8:7

S ome of the sins we commit occur when we are flying solo. We're alone and nobody knows what we're up to. But a good many of them are done in tandem with someone else. Having an affair, which may be the biggest shame-producing sin of all time, is an example. In that situation, you wrestle not only with your feelings of guilt and shame toward yourself, but also with your anger against the person you sinned with. And it's possible that those feelings could be intense, especially if you feel that person took advantage of you in some way or coaxed you into the situation that devastated your life.

~ "He only cared about himself, not me."

~ "I said I didn't want to, but she kept pressuring me."

~ "He used his authority over me to make me feel like I had to."

Sometimes statements like these are just excuses, but sometimes they are true. And when they are true, they are hard to deal with.

In her book, *5 Minutes with Jesus*, Sheila Walsh talks about how hard it is to forgive people who have deeply hurt you. She shares how she started carrying a small rock with her to remind her of what Jesus said in John 8:7, that only people who are without sin should hold grudges or throw stones.

At the time she wrote the book, she had been carrying the rock 28 years.

If you're having trouble forgiving someone you feel is at least partly responsible for your shame, maybe you should head outdoors right now and find a small rock. Pick it up, dust it off, and drop it in your purse or pocket. Let it be your reminder to let your anger go and move on.

Forgiveness is not a matter of reason; it's a matter of obedience.

Sheila Walsh

For Further Reflection

Psalm 37:8; Proverbs 19:11

TODAY'S PRAYER

Father in heaven, cleanse me of these feelings of anger I have toward the person who was involved in my sin. Help me to understand that we are both broken and in desperate need of your grace and mercy.

God Speaks

Ask and it will be given to you; seek and you will find;
knock and the door will be opened to you.

MATTHEW 7:7 NIV

The silent treatment.

It's that deafening silence you get from someone after you've messed up. You might think it would be considered a good thing. After all, "silent" means no one is yelling at you. But just about everybody who gets the silent treatment will tell you that they'd rather them say something—anything! Silence can be very difficult to deal with when you're feeling guilty.

This is especially true in our relationship with God. Most people who've sinned spectacularly and are dealing with shame crave a word from the Lord, some indication that he hasn't abandoned them. What's dangerous is when they are so desperate for some message from God that they start seeing messages from God everywhere they look.

In today's verse, God promises that there will be no silent treatment when we come to him; he will respond to us. But he doesn't speak to us in ways so unusual and mysterious that it will require us to decipher every little thing that happens; he speaks to us through his Word. This means that if you want to hear from God, you need to open your Bible and start reading. Everything he wants you to know about how he feels, what he thinks, and what you should do is in there.

When navigating the aftermath of sin, people will have plenty to say to you. It's what God says that should concern you the most.

What if God isn't saying anything to us because he's already said it?

Bob Goff

For Further Reflection

Jeremiah 33:3; John 10:27

TODAY'S PRAYER

Father, thank you for your Word.
Thank you for speaking to every issue I face.
Help me to realize that my spiritual health
will rise or fall according to the amount
of time I spend listening to you.

Choices

You will always harvest what you plant.

GALATIANS 6:7

Ever wonder how many choices you make each day?

Psychology Today reports that the average person makes about 35,000 choices every day. If a person spends seven hours a day sleeping, that leaves about 2,000 choices per hour while they are awake. That's about one decision every two seconds.

Makes you feel a little tired, doesn't it?

The more important question is, how many *bad* decisions do you make each day? Unsurprisingly, the quality of your life is going to fluctuate depending on your answer. Perhaps the reason you're battling shame is because you made a bad decision. Maybe you made quite a few of them and they finally caught up with you. So how are you going to improve your decision-making?

A key to making consistently good choices is to decide as many things as possible ahead of time, especially things to do with faith and morality. For example, if you're married, you don't wait until an attractive coworker flirts with you to decide how you're going to respond to flirtations. If you decide in the moment, you increase your chances of making a bad choice. You must settle the matter ahead of time.

Be like the farmer who knows that his harvest hinges on what he does long before the harvest season arrives.

One of the greatest discoveries of my life as a pastor who counsels was the discovery that people are what they have decided to be.

Stephen Brown

For Further Reflection

Hosea 10:12; Proverbs 1:31

TODAY'S PRAYER

Dear Lord, my choices have not always been good. Thank you for loving me anyway. Help me to be more thoughtful in the future and to make my most important decisions ahead of time, guided by Scripture.

End or Mend?

[There is] a time to tear and a time to mend.

ECCLESIASTES 3:7

Four things can happen to a relationship.

- ∾ It can thrive.
- ∾ It can stay the same.
- ∾ It can deteriorate.
- ∾ It can end.

When a relationship is the source of trouble in your life, it needs to end. Maybe the person you're in the relationship with is a bad influence on you. Maybe he or she has different values and pressures you to compromise your convictions, or drags you down emotionally. If you're battling shame, it's quite possible that you can trace the source of your trouble back to your involvement with someone who is not good for you.

But even when we know a relationship is unhealthy, we often have a hard time ending it. Part of our reluctance might be our belief that God can change people. Another part certainly has to do with how painful it is to let go of someone who has meant a lot to us and with whom we have a lot of history. Even if it's painful history, it's still shared experience, which can have a very bonding effect.

But as today's verse says, there's "a time to tear." There is a time when the only sensible option is to end the relationship and move on. Whatever pain or disappointment you feel in that decision will be more than made up for by the lessening of pain and trouble in your life. The world is full of people who never found happiness and peace until they were set free from the bonds of an unhealthy association.

Endings are the reason you are not married to your prom date nor still working in your first job. Without the ability to do endings well, we flounder, stay stuck, and fail to reach our goals and dreams.

Henry Cloud

For Further Reflection
Matthew 10:14; Hebrews 12:1

TODAY'S PRAYER

Lord Jesus, help me not to be dependent on anyone but you. Make it known to me when I am clinging to a relationship that needs to be ended—and give me the courage to do it.

Permissible vs. Beneficial

You say, "I am allowed to do anything"—
but not everything is beneficial.

1 CORINTHIANS 10:23

In 2019, 25.8 percent of people 18 and older admitted they had engaged in binge drinking, according to the National Institute on Alcohol Abuse and Alcoholism. Binge drinking is defined as consuming large amounts of alcohol in a short period, usually five drinks in a two-hour period for a man and four drinks in a two-hour period for a woman.

Binge drinking is dangerous for more reasons than can be listed here, but a couple are worth noting. First, binge drinking severely affects your judgment and reflexes, making it likely that you will do something to endanger yourself or others, or at the very least embarrass yourself. Second, regular binge drinking adversely affects virtually all your vital organs, making it likely that you will develop severe health problems.

However, binge drinking is not illegal. It's often called "partying" by people who do it regularly, and it is particularly popular among college students.

Generally, it's not the illegal things we do that ruin our lives; it's the permissible things that are counterproductive to our happiness. Binge drinking is only one example. There are countless others, such as flirting with a married coworker, working 60 hours a week, or overeating. All of these actions are permissible, but none of them are beneficial.

Maybe the shame you're battling right now does not stem from an illegal act. Maybe you did something that's acceptable in our culture. Let this be a teaching moment. Doing what's permissible might make you popular, but a higher standard is needed if you really want to be happy.

Cultural permissibility has never been the benchmark for God's vision for a beautiful life. You were never meant to be common.

Daniel Fusco

For Further Reflection
Deuteronomy 30:19; Psalm 119:30

TODAY'S PRAYER

Gracious Father, give me a passion,
not for the permissible, but for the righteous.
In this fallen world, help me to be more
concerned about standing out than fitting in.

When Is Sin Not a Sin?

*If we claim to be without sin, we deceive ourselves
and the truth is not in us.*

1 JOHN 1:8 NIV

You've heard the children's joke: "When is a door not a door? When it's ajar, of course."

So, when is a sin not a sin?

When we convince ourselves that it isn't.

One of the most astounding abilities people have is to rewrite history, or at least reframe it to leave a different impression. We've seen politicians play spin-doctor, but so do people who've been caught in sin. The first step is to change the wording. Dispense with lingo such as "sin," "disobedience," and "unfaithful" and start using words and phrases such as "stumble," "error in judgment," and "moment of weakness." And if you really want to inspire sympathy in people around you, talk about how you were under attack from Satan. Who doesn't feel sorry for someone under attack?

After shifting your language as you creatively rewrite the event, next adjust your attitude. Instead of acting contrite, you must act wounded. That person you cheated with? He seduced you in a weak moment. That drunk driving charge you got? You had *no idea* the punch bowl at the party was spiked.

See how it works?

Oh wait, you probably already know all this. You've seen events masterfully reframed—and probably done it yourself.

In today's verse, John is saying, "Don't even think about trying to excuse yourself. The only person you'll be fooling is yourself."

Overcoming shame requires brutal honesty. Because no matter how skillfully you spin what you did, deep in your heart you'll know you're a liar.

We are all very skilled at presenting the logic of the argument that what we have done says more about the flawed people and dysfunctional things around us than it does about us.

Paul David Tripp

For Further Reflection

Psalm 24:3–4; Proverbs 10:9

TODAY'S PRAYER

O God, search my heart to see if there is any dishonesty in me. Convict me of the sin of trying to pretend I am a victim when I know full well I'm not.

First Place

Seek the Kingdom of God above all else,
and live righteously, and he will give you
everything you need.

MATTHEW 6:33

The sports page is one of the most read sections of the newspaper (or news website). Many readers want to check out the standings first, to learn how their team fared in the latest game and whether they hung onto or moved any closer to first place.

First place matters in sports. It matters in our Christian walk, too. Jesus made this clear when he spoke our verse for today. He said that God's provision in our lives depends on us making his Kingdom our priority. Notice there's no qualifier. He doesn't say, "Seek the Kingdom of God above all else on Sundays." That's what many people do. He also doesn't say, "Seek the Kingdom above all else when you're feeling shame and are trying to get back on God's good side." Many people do that, too.

He's talking about seeking God's Kingdom every minute of every day. What does this mean? It means putting God in first place—as King of your life. It means considering how every decision you make will affect God's purposes and your own Christian witness. And then you make your choice accordingly, even if it's uncomfortable. That's really the key. Anyone can seek the Kingdom of God when it's comfortable. The real test is what we do when it isn't.

The person who does not seek the kingdom first does not seek it at all.

Richard J. Foster

For Further Reflection

Matthew 5:6; Exodus 20:3

TODAY'S PRAYER

Lord Jesus, you made my life's mission clear with these words. Help me not to shy away from the challenge they contain, but to embrace it and make it my life's passion.

The Cock-Sure Christian

If you think you are standing strong,
be careful not to fall.

1 CORINTHIANS 10:12

I n 1611, Francis Grose wrote *The Classic Dictionary of the Vulgar Tongue*, in which he attempted to explain the meaning and origins of many less-than-classy words. He said the word "cock-sure," which means overconfident or arrogant, referred to the cocking mechanism in a musket. If he'd had the internet, he would have discovered that his theory couldn't possibly be true because the word shows up in literature many years before the musket was invented. Most scholars believe the word refers to the strutting rooster, which can always be counted on to crow in the morning.

Regardless of where the word came from, it is an important one to consider as you think about the battle to overcome shame. When Christians are cock-sure, they stand a much greater chance of being attacked by Satan—and a much greater chance of getting hurt. In fact, I doubt that anything inspires and empowers our enemy as does our arrogance. Whatever you did that brought great shame into your life, it likely came from pride. Perhaps you skipped along the boundary of sin and thought you could handle it, only to tumble over the line.

Remember Peter's boast? "Lord, even if I have to die with you, I will never deny you!" (Matthew 26:35). Pretty cock-sure, wouldn't you say? And sure enough, he failed that very night.

But as much as Satan is inspired and motivated by our arrogance, he is intimidated by our humble devotion to God. He knows that a Holy Spirit-powered Christian is well-protected from every missile in his arsenal.

Satan trembles when he sees the weakest saint upon his knees.

William Cowper

For Further Reflection

Jeremiah 17:9; Psalm 73:26

TODAY'S PRAYER

Loving Father, forgive me for foolishly thinking I could play with fire and not get burned. Help me to remember that I am never stronger than when I realize how weak I am.

Red-Handed

The Pharisees brought a woman who had been caught in the act of adultery.

JOHN 8:3

"Caught in the act."

We call it being caught "red-handed." It's a term that originated hundreds of years ago and it refers to a murderer being caught with blood on his hands. Of course, a novelist can easily take a suspect with blood on his hands and flip the details upside down and make him innocent. But in real life, being caught red-handed generally offers no way out.

The woman in our verse for today was caught red-handed committing a capital offense. In that culture, people who committed adultery could be stoned. The Pharisees, who hated Jesus, cared nothing about her life or her soul, they merely wanted to leverage her sin to try to make Jesus look bad.

But let's forget about the Pharisees and Jesus for a moment and zero in on the woman. It pains us to think about her being caught red-handed. How awful. How humiliating. The love or desire she must have felt when the act began quickly morphed into terror when the door was flung open. Still, I believe it was the best thing that could have happened.

If she had only been rumored to have committed adultery, she likely would have been tempted to lie and make excuses and try to save herself. The fact that she was caught red-handed means she had no option except to stand broken before Jesus.

More people need to stand broken before Jesus.

If you want to overcome the shame you're feeling, *you* need to stand broken before Jesus. If you were caught red-handed, don't bemoan the fact; thank God for it. Yes, it was humiliating, but it might be the thing that kept you from compounding your sin by trying to deny it.

Contrary to what we would expect, brokenness is the pathway to blessing!

Nancy Leigh DeMoss

For Further Reflection

Matthew 5:3-4; John 12:24

TODAY'S PRAYER

Lord Jesus, may I never forget the grace you showed to the woman caught red-handed. May it always remind me to bring my sin and my brokenness to you instead of trying to defend myself.

Wounds

Oh LORD, if you heal me,
I will be truly healed.

JEREMIAH 17:14

If you've done much fishing, you know it's not unusual to catch a fish that has wounds and scars. Sometimes they're so beaten up it's hard to imagine what happened or how they survived. Life underwater is not easy.

Life above water is not easy either. We coined the term "walking wounded" to refer to people who make their way through life battered, beaten, and scarred. Sometimes it seems there's no one in the world who *isn't* walking around wounded.

Few people would argue that the worst wounds are self-inflicted. If someone else attacks and hurts me, I can process that by understanding that there are bad people in the world. But when my wound is self-inflicted, I have some much deeper and more complicated issues to deal with. It's basically the difference between looking out a window and looking in a mirror. Give me a window any day over a mirror. Looking in a mirror is always hard.

The good news is that God can heal all our wounds, self-inflicted and otherwise. But that doesn't mean you won't have any lingering effects. Healing is not the same as removing the consequences of your sin. You may have to live with some of the results of what you've done the rest of your life. But at least you can be freed from the guilt and the shame, which will enable you to move on with your life with joy in your heart and be a witness to others.

Those aren't warts, beloved. Just a little scar tissue from wounds that God has healed.

Liz Curtis Higgs

For Further Reflection

Psalm 147:3; Jeremiah 30:17

TODAY'S PRAYER

Dear Father, I know there is nothing to be gained by pretending I don't hurt. Help me to bring my wounds to you for the healing that only you can give.

Honoring God

*Put on every piece of God's armor so you will be able
to resist the enemy in the time of evil.*

EPHESIANS 6:13

Consider for a moment the servant of God who has fallen into sin and is battling shame. Maybe it's you. Perhaps you have been a pastor, an associate pastor, a Bible teacher, or the leader of a great ministry in your church. You had the respect of people because you earned it with faithful service over a period of years. But now you feel all is lost. The church has removed you from your post. How will you ever be able to honor God with your talents in the future? Won't people think of your sin every time they look at you?

First, you must stop thinking in terms of *your* service and *your* image and *your* ministry. Thinking primarily of yourself is likely how you got into trouble in the first place. Set your focus on God. Instead of worrying about what people will think of you, it's time to make what he thinks your priority.

God is not thinking about your future in ministry—he's focused on your heart. Whether you ever preach another sermon or teach another class pales in comparison to whether you learn to live in submission to his will. *That's* what he's concerned about.

God is best honored, not in the dazzling display of our talents in his church, but in the daily surrender of our hearts to his will. Even if you never serve in a leadership position in church again, you will honor God to his heart's content if you just submit yourself to his will from this day forward.

Every time we resist the slightest temptation, we honor God.

Robert J. Morgan

For Further Reflection

1 Corinthians 10:31; 1 Corinthians 6:19

TODAY'S PRAYER

Lord, thank you for the gifts and abilities you've given me, but help me to remember that they mean little if I don't back them up with obedience.

It's Harder Than It Looks

Humble yourselves before God.

JAMES 4:7

H ave you ever thought about what you would do if you could be God for a day? Some people came up with amusing answers:

- ∾ "I would make donuts a health food."

- ∾ "I would make pimples invisible."

- ∾ "I would make math easy for everybody."

It's a fun question that often produces humorous responses. What's not so funny is that many people *do* try to be God, at least as far as their own lives are concerned. They like to sit in the driver's seat and steer, going where they want at whatever speed they choose. They don't mind God sitting in the passenger seat, or better yet in the back. They like for him to be on stand-by, a kind of safety net in case things get dicey. But mainly they prefer for him to keep quiet unless he's called on.

No believer ever wants to admit to having this attitude. But when you look at how people live, how can you deny it's true? If you have committed a serious sin that has filled you with shame, it's very likely that you were running the show, calling your own shots, doing what you felt like doing without regard for God. Maybe there were moments when he tried to get your attention or lead you in a different direction. I'm guessing that, metaphorically speaking, you told him to pipe down, that you'd call him when you needed him.

And now you need him. Big time.

You're not in charge. This is a critical truth we all need to come to grips with. No human has ever tried to be God without failing miserably. Moving forward, let God be God and you just be you.

We don't live very long before we find that we would like to be our own gods.

Eugene Peterson

For Further Reflection
1 Peter 5:6; Luke 14:11

TODAY'S PRAYER

Father in heaven, I have made a mess of my life. Please forgive me for trying to do for myself what only you can do. May my sin be a constant reminder that I need to humble myself before you.

Make It Personal

For we live by believing and not by seeing.

2 CORINTHIANS 5:7

Many Christians settle into a way of thinking that is counterproductive to healing and restoration when we sin. It happens without us realizing it, and when it rears its ugly head, it can be quite troublesome. It's the tendency to think of Jesus as *the* Savior rather than *my* Savior.

There's an old song by Andre Crouch that talks about Jesus being the answer "for the world today." We look at the condition of the world and we think, "Yes, the world really needs Jesus." We support missions in an effort to carry the Gospel into all the world. But when we fall into sin, somehow that Savior who is everything the world needs seems far away and unreachable.

For some reason, it's easier to think about Jesus as a corporate Savior than a personal Savior. Perhaps it's because we know how dark and corrupt our own hearts are. We know how often we think things we shouldn't think and do things we shouldn't do. The world's sins can be easily painted with a broad brush, but our own sins are itemized on a rap sheet that horrifies us. It's hard for us to imagine Jesus not being repulsed when he looks at us. We think, "If I were Jesus, I wouldn't want anything to do with me."

But check out our verse for today. We live by believing, and not by seeing. Yes, you *see* your rap sheet. You know every bullet point on it. But you *believe* the blood of Christ is sufficient to erase every one of those sins. This is a hurdle you must get over...not just thinking about Jesus as *the* Savior but embracing him as *your* Savior.

Take your human feelings, multiply them exponentially into infinity, and you will have a hint of the love of God revealed by and in Jesus Christ. With a strong affirmation of our goodness and a gentle understanding of our weakness, God is loving us—you and me—this moment, just as we are and not as we should be.

Brennan Manning

For Further Reflection

John 1:12; John 3:16

TODAY'S PRAYER

Lord Jesus, I have talked of your love,
sung of your love, and listened to
grand sermons about your love.
Help me now to embrace it and truly believe
that it's not just for others, but for me too.

The Unseen

Faith shows the reality of what we hope for;
it is the evidence of things we cannot see.

HEBREWS 11:1

Have you ever been to a Broadway musical? If so, you probably watched a group of 20 or 30 people act, sing, and dance their way through the show. But if you thumbed through the Playbill you received when you walked in, you saw that there were a lot more than 20 or 30 people involved in the show. There was an orchestra in the pit, stagehands, and wardrobe and lighting people. In other words, you didn't see all kinds of behind-the-scenes activity that was essential to the show's success.

So often in life, it's the stuff we don't see that makes all the difference.

That brilliant professor who impacted you in a powerful way? You didn't see the countless hours of study and hard work that made him what he is.

That vaccine that was injected into your arm to protect you from COVID-19? You didn't see the long hours and diligent research that produced it.

Much of what God does is unseen too.

Take, for example, the sin that brought shame into your life. Maybe you assume that God just stood back and let it happen. Have you considered the possibility that he cushioned your fall? Take the classic case of a man who crashes his car while driving drunk. The doctor later says, "There's no way he should have survived that crash. He should be dead." Are you willing to consider that God himself was at the scene of *your* "crash," providing protection, sparing you (and maybe others) greater harm, and giving you another chance? Could it be that your situation would be far worse without your loving heavenly Father's unseen hand at work?

Periodically, as I fall asleep, I like to thank God for the things He did for me today that I am unaware of.

Joseph M. Stowell

For Further Reflection

Hebrews 11:6; 2 Corinthians 5:7

TODAY'S PRAYER

Father in heaven, I've always believed you work in mysterious ways. Your Word makes it clear that you do. Thank you for the good things you do in my life that are mysterious and unseen, that bless me in ways I'm not even aware of.

Rinse and Repeat

So he went to pray a third time,
saying the same things again.

MATTHEW 26:44

"Rinse and repeat" is a common idiom we use when trying to impress on someone the importance of repetition. It's a saying that pokes fun at shampoo manufacturers who put the instruction on their bottles: "Lather, rinse, and repeat." The joke is that if people actually followed those instructions, they would end up washing their hair over and over again until they ran out of shampoo.

In some areas of life, "rinse and repeat" is good advice. In today's verse, we see Jesus praying a third time and saying the same things he said the first two times. Clearly, he was a believer in praying the same prayers repeatedly. Paul must have been, too, because he instructed us to "never stop praying." That doesn't mean to keep praying 24/7, but to never give up on a prayer just because it isn't answered.

But in other areas, the "rinse and repeat" approach can be counterproductive, or even harmful. Binge watching questionable TV shows, constantly obsessing over social media, compulsive Amazon shopping, or even overworking day after day can cause you to lose sight of what's truly important.

Reflect on the reason you're battling shame right now. Could it be that the seeds of your sin were planted in the soil of some habit or pattern of behavior that was unhealthy? If so, have you made that correction? Even if you feel sorry for your sin and are trying to do better, you must establish new, healthier habits if you want to avoid similar failures in the future.

Only when a hamster steps off his wheel can he actually get anywhere.

Robin Dance

For Further Reflection

1 Timothy 4:7; 2 Peter 2:19

TODAY'S PRAYER

Dear Lord, touch my eyes that I may see the deeper reality of what I am doing with my time. Help me not to waste it, but to invest it in those things that are going to bring me closer to you.

DAY 37

What Are You?

See how very much our Father loves us, for he calls us his children, and that is what we are!

1 JOHN 3:1

No one wants to be labeled. But most of us label others to some extent, even simply by placing people into categories such as "soccer mom," "millennial," "cancer survivor," or "vegan." Some labels might not bother us, but others sting when they're thrown our way. One is the word 'hypocrite.' If I'm called a hypocrite, I have to stop and ask myself if there's something in my life that would give credence to the charge.

If you've done something terrible and are now battling to overcome shame, someone has probably called you a hypocrite. And it probably stung worse than any yellow jacket you ever tangled with. You probably hung your head and agreed. You probably felt like you deserved it and that people would see the word emblazoned across your forehead for the rest of your life.

Understand two things. First, these thoughts and feelings come from your enemy, Satan, who is your accuser. He loves nothing more than to try to destroy your hope by constantly throwing your failures in your face.

Second, you are not what Satan says you are; you are what God says you are. God has slapped a label on you too, and it's not "hypocrite." It's "son" or "daughter." He calls you his child, and while he may be saddened by your disobedience, he would no more disown you than you would disown your own children when they mess up.

Don't believe the lies that you are defined by your successes or your failures. You are defined by Jesus, and He calls you beloved.

Bob Goff

For Further Reflection

Romans 8:16; Galatians 3:26

TODAY'S PRAYER

Lord, thank you for adopting me,
for welcoming me into your family…
and for not kicking me out when I sinned.
Help me to embrace the fact that I am your
child, and to live like it from this day forward.

A Great Opportunity

Let your good deeds shine out for all to see.

MATTHEW 5:16

According to the Food and Agriculture Organization of the United Nations, about a third of the food the world produces never gets eaten. There are many reasons for this, but one is that many fruits and vegetables simply don't look "presentable enough." They are deemed too undersized, oddly shaped, or damaged to be of value, so they are thrown away. In the United States, the statistics are higher. By some estimates, about 40 percent of the food in America goes uneaten.

When you sin in a way that leaves you broken and deeply ashamed, you might feel you've become worthless to God and could just as well be thrown away. But nothing could be further from the truth. When you have been broken by sin you have a unique opportunity to offer the world a powerful witness. If you genuinely repent, submit to the Lord, and change your ways, people will see the power of God demonstrated in you in ways they might never have otherwise.

This does not mean Christians should go out and sin spectacularly so they can have a greater witness, but it does mean you can still be useful to God. In the Bible, many people (like David and Peter) achieved great things for God after committing terrible sins. Just as an undersized banana or a weirdly shaped tomato can still feed someone who's hungry, so your less-than-perfect life can still be an inspiration to someone who needs hope.

You can argue with ideas, you can challenge beliefs, you can roll your eyes in weariness at new programs and fads in the church, but when someone's life is drastically and permanently changed, people have no recourse but to pay attention.

Dan Schaeffer

For Further Reflection

2 Corinthians 5:17; Ezekiel 36:26

TODAY'S PRAYER

Dear Jesus, thank you for dying on the cross for my sins…for making it possible for me to be a new creature. Help me now to live in a way that gives hope to others who have sinned and feel worthless.

Why God Is
So Good to You

The Lord will not abandon his people,
because that would dishonor his great name.

1 SAMUEL 12:22

Have you ever experienced a random act of kindness? Maybe it was a person you barely knew, or someone you had nothing in common with, or someone of a very different age, or someone who ought to be a rival. It might have made you a little uneasy or questioning whether the person had an ulterior motive.

Sometimes people wonder why God is so good to them. "All I've ever done is disappoint him," they say. "How could he still love me? Why would he keep blessing me? It just doesn't make sense."

It doesn't make sense if you think purely in terms of his righteousness and your failures. But it does make sense if you take yourself out of the equation and just think about God. Our verse for today tells us that God doesn't turn his back on his people, not because we're so wonderful, but because his name and reputation are at stake. If he were to suddenly get fed up with us and abandon us, then his integrity and the truthfulness of his Word would suddenly be shot. He would no longer be the God whose Word never fails.

The good news here is that God's love doesn't depend on your performance. If you fail to be perfectly sweet and irresistible, God isn't suddenly going to say, "Okay, that does it. You're off my list. I'm not going to help you anymore." Quite the contrary. He is going to love you and work in your life as long as you will let him...because he's God and that's what he does.

God's allegiance to his own name is the foundation of his faithfulness to us.

John Piper

For Further Reflection

Exodus 34:6; Psalm 145:9

TODAY'S PRAYER

Father in heaven, you are far better to me than I deserve, and I thank you. Give me peace in those moments when Satan tries to make me believe that you have abandoned me.

Step By Step

Mark out a straight path for your feet;
stay on the safe path.

PROVERBS 4:26

You've heard the old joke: "How do you eat an elephant? One bite at a time."

Such a silly joke actually has serious relevance to the Christian life. People could well ask, "How do you live a faithful Christian life?" In a permissive culture where Christians and unbelievers often live almost identical lifestyles, eating an elephant might seem like an easier task. But the answer is simple: You live a faithful Christian life one step at a time.

Throughout the Bible are references to walking with God. Walking is a step-by-step proposition. In our verse for today we're told that we need to mark out a straight path, not for our horses or bicycles or automobiles, but for our feet. Again, it's the picture of a step-by-step process.

Step-by-step is how we grow in our faith and get closer to God, but it's also how we wander from him. If you have sinned deeply and are now struggling with shame, you likely did not make a single disobedient decision. Rather, you took one step off the straight path, then another, and another, until you found yourself in a place you never imagined.

Many people stray a little off the straight path and feel no sense of alarm. They think, "I'm close to the path. I can

still see the path. I can step back onto the path at any time."
What they fail to realize is that they will grow comfortable
being one step off the path, and then two won't seem like a
big deal. And when they adjust to being two steps off, three
won't seem to matter.

Mark out a straight path for your feet and stay on it.
Otherwise, it's only a matter of time before you'll have a new
load of shame to deal with.

Parents have always known that one thing leads to another.

John White

For Further Reflection

Psalm 5:8; Psalm 25:4

TODAY'S PRAYER

Father, help me to appreciate the wisdom of
living a step-by-step life. Show me the straight
path and do whatever it takes to steer me back
onto it when I begin to stray.

Boredom

This, too, is meaningless—like chasing the wind.

ECCLESIASTES 2:26

E very parent in the world knows that boredom is one of the main causes of mischief in children. Kids who are bored have decided that their toys and whatever else has been provided to entertain them is no longer fun, so they begin looking for something new and different to do, and often it ends up being something outside the boundaries their parents have set. Somehow a boundary just screams "Bor-ing!" but what's outside the boundary appears exciting and fascinating.

Not much changes when we get older.

In a world full of gadgets and gizmos created for the sole purpose of entertaining us, it's hard to imagine boredom being a problem, but it is. People seem bored with their careers and their marriages, which could explain why so many individuals jump from one job to another, or one relationship to another. People who have affairs confess they were bored, that the excitement had gone out of their marriage, causing them to look for something (or someone) outside the boundary...someone new and exciting.

Is that what happened to you?

If so, to keep it from happening again you need to address why you were bored. Here's a secret: boredom happens in your own head. When two people look at the same thing—

like Mount Rushmore or a Broadway show—and one is thrilled while the other is bored, the difference is not in what they're seeing but what they're *thinking* about what they're seeing.

Next time you become bored with your spouse, examine your thoughts before you blame the other person. Do the hard work of tracking where your thoughts have come from and where they are going.

To be bored to death is a form of suicide.

Frederick Buechner

For Further Reflection

Proverbs 18:9; Proverbs 19:15

TODAY'S PRAYER

God of Creation, you have filled the world with wonderful things to be enjoyed. Forgive me when I become bored with your blessings and start looking around for a cheap distraction.

Own It

He beat his chest in sorrow, saying,
"O God, be merciful to me, for I am a sinner."

Luke 18:13

As you might expect, the Central Intelligence Agency is good at being cagey. Their PR people have been trained to give answers to questions without really giving answers to questions. For example, the following is an actual response the CIA has given: "We can neither confirm nor deny the existence of the information requested, but, hypothetically, if such data were to exist, the subject matter would be classified and could not be disclosed." Obviously, the CIA is not going to admit to anything.

Sometimes we're just as good at being cagey. We'll parse words and split hairs to keep from admitting our bad behavior. Sometimes we'll rewrite history in our favor—or simply deny everything, especially when we know there's no hard evidence to prove us wrong.

This kind of behavior is to be expected from unbelievers, but Christians must do better. In fact, the extent of your recovery from a shameful moral failure will be determined by your level of transparency. As long as your goal is to mitigate your guilt and win sympathy, you will never be fully whole. You might fool some people, but in your heart you'll know the truth. And some day you'll look into a mirror and feel contempt for the person you see.

Remember this: People who try to be cagey are often exposed eventually anyway and viewed with scorn. People who admit their sin are usually forgiven and respected for their honesty. Which do you want to be?

Before you take any steps to break a habit, you have to first own it.

Steve Poe

For Further Reflection

Psalm 69:5; Psalm 38:18

TODAY'S PRAYER

Lord, help me to be honest, to see the futility of trying to be cagey about my sin. Give me the courage to own it and accept the consequences so I can put it behind me and begin to rebuild my life with your help.

The Critical Question

You don't love me or each other as you did at first!

REVELATION 2:4

We make assumptions all the time and much of our behavior depends on them being true. For example:

~ We assume restaurants serve food that is safe to eat.

~ We assume airline pilots are competent and experienced.

~ We assume we won't have all the possible side effects that are listed on our medications.

~ And we assume that people who go to church love Jesus.

While these things are mostly safe to assume, we've all seen or heard exceptions: the restaurant that is shut down for unsanitary conditions, the pilot who is fired for being drunk, the medication that practically kills someone, and the churchgoer who doesn't appear to love Jesus...at least not as much as he loves the world.

In today's verse, our Lord takes the church in Ephesus to task for their dwindling love for him and each other. Think about yourself. Has your love for Jesus waned? Are you less faithful and committed than you used to be? Is it possible the reason you're now battling shame is because you drifted from Jesus and started to do things you once would have avoided? Have you lowered your standards as the distance between you and Jesus has grown?

If so, you don't need anything as much as you need to spend some time with Jesus. You don't need to read a book or go to counseling or even go to church as much as you need to lock yourself in a room with your Bible and seek the Lord through his Word and prayer. Reconnect with him and rediscover why you loved him in the first place. The most critical question for any of us is: Where do I stand with Jesus?

It's frightening to think that love for God is a rare quality, even among churchgoers.

Robert J. Morgan

For Further Reflection

Hebrews 2:1; Hebrews 10:23

TODAY'S PRAYER

Lord Jesus, I know that getting myself right does not depend on you coming back to me, but on me coming back to you. Awaken in me the passion for you that I once found so thrilling, that I may serve you again with a full heart.

Unguarded

*Come close to God, and God
will come close to you.*

JAMES 4:8

W hat's the difference between a friend and an
acquaintance? I dare say it's honesty.

When an acquaintance asks how you're doing, you respond
with a preprogrammed, "Good, and you?" But when a friend
asks, you're apt to go on a five-minute rant about how your
neighbor was playing loud music half the night or your boss
just assigned you to a project you're going to hate, or your
arthritis has been killing you lately. It's natural to open up to
a friend but be more guarded with acquaintances.

So think about your prayer life.

Do you treat God as a friend or an acquaintance?

Do you open up to him and pour out your heart, or do you
take a more guarded approach?

There is a way of praying that is very formal and dignified.
It uses words that are rarely heard outside of church, like
"bestow," for example: *Thank you, Lord, for the blessings
you have bestowed on me.* There's nothing wrong with this,
of course, except that maybe the formality is keeping you
from really opening up to God. Perhaps in your desire to
be proper, you're bottling up the scream in your heart that
needs to be released.

God wants you to draw near to him, and that means letting down your guard and telling him how you really feel. He would much rather you release the scream that's stuck in your throat than pray a pretty little prayer that is more about decorum than honesty. When you do finally get real before God, I suspect he'll smile and think, "Okay, now we're getting somewhere."

To be God's friend, you must be honest to God, sharing your true feelings, not what you think you ought to feel or say.

Rick Warren

For Further Reflection

Hebrews 10:22; Psalm 91:1

TODAY'S PRAYER

Father in heaven, I have become so accustomed to hiding my struggles from people that sometimes I forget and hide them from you too. Forgive me, and help me to be more honest and unguarded when I approach your throne.

God Gets You

You know my thoughts, even when I'm far away.

PSALM 139:2

Vincent Van Gogh produced over 2,000 paintings that sell for millions of dollars today. But did you know that during his lifetime he lived in poverty and only sold one painting? He also suffered from severe depression. Imagine the people in his orbit, walking by him every day and not giving a moment's notice. They looked right past him, maybe right through him. They certainly didn't "get" him at all.

Have you ever felt as though nobody understands you?

Maybe that feeling is part of the reason you veered into sin. Perhaps the frustration you feel with your spouse or your parents or your boss or your coworkers left you feeling isolated. Maybe you felt as though there was no one you could talk to about your feelings, at least no one who would understand. Often, people have affairs, not because they're desperate for sex, but because they're desperate to be in the company of someone who at least pretends to understand them.

The good news is that God gets you. He gets you the way a creator gets his creation. He made you. He knows what you're made of and how you work. You can have thoughts and feelings that don't make sense to you, but you can't have thoughts and feelings that don't make sense to him.

When people are battling shame, they tend to look for something that will help, something like this devotional, for example. That's good, but maybe it's not just some*thing* you need, but some*one*. Don't let a preacher or an author or a book or a podcast take the place of God. *He's* the one who really gets you.

One reason I have maintained my walk with God is that no one else, not even my beloved family or my close and loyal friends, really understands me.

Anne Graham Lotz

For Further Reflection

Psalm 44:21; Jeremiah 17:10

TODAY'S PRAYER

Lord, when I think of how many people I don't understand, I can't be surprised when people don't understand me. Thank you for your understanding; it is a rare and precious gift.

Your Next Step

*Your word is a lamp to guide my feet
and a light for my path.*

PSALM 119:105

One of the most painful things in life is a stubbed toe. You're gliding happily through a room barefooted, and suddenly you're hopping on one foot, screaming and seeing stars. In that moment, no pain in the world can compare.

The reason toes get stubbed is because people are not looking at what's right in front of them. They're looking farther down the path. Maybe the reason shame entered your life is because you weren't paying enough attention to what was right in front of you. Maybe you were so focused on what you wanted to do in the future that you forgot to consider what you were doing in the present.

The task that's right in front of you is the most essential. Yes, it's important to have goals and dreams. But if you don't properly handle your current roles and responsibilities, you could easily disqualify yourself for something bigger later. Unplanned pregnancies, drug busts, drunk driving charges, and adulterous relationships are just a few situations often triggered by momentary lapses in judgment that spiral unchecked, producing long-term consequences.

In today's verse, David reminds us that the Word of God is a light that shines on our path. The picture is of a torch that lights a person's next step, illuminating what's directly in front of him. No great accomplishment ever happens in one fell swoop. A dream is achieved by many single steps properly taken over a long period of time.

You next step is always the most important!

The Enemy is trying to get you off assignment. He wants to distract you with something that God is not emphasizing in your life so that you will miss what God wants to teach you in that moment.

Banning Liebscher

For Further Reflection

Galatians 5:16; Psalm 119:133

TODAY'S PRAYER

Dear Lord, it's so hard for me to live in the moment when much of what I dream for seems farther down the road. Help me to concentrate more on today, to make sure my next step is a good one.

Hearing

He who has ears to hear, let him hear.

MARK 4:9 NIV

According to the U.S. Department of Health and Human Services, about 37.5 million Americans report some trouble hearing. About 28.8 million of those could benefit from hearing aids, but only about two thirds have ever used a hearing aid. It's good to keep in mind that maybe the person who seems to be ignoring you might not be rude but hard of hearing.

How's *your* hearing—not literally but figuratively? How willing are you to really hear what's being said to you? Think about the sin you committed that has brought shame into your life and caused you to turn to this book. Was it something you'd been warned about? Are there people close to you—maybe your parents or a spouse or a friend—who saw you edging closer and closer to trouble and tried to warn you? Had you heard multiple sermons on the subject?

The world is full of people who make eye contact, listen, and nod, but don't really hear what's being said. Their ears work just fine, but the truth that goes in hits a roadblock on its way to their hearts. When this happens, willfulness is usually the problem. The person's self-will has been made the boss and flexes its muscle, blocking out any idea or notion it doesn't like. Is this what happened to you?

Your future health and happiness—maybe even your salvation—depends on your willingness to clear out that roadblock and let God's truth penetrate your heart.

It's amazing that a man can't hear his wife talking when she's across the breakfast table from him—but he can hear the faint sound of gobbling two ridges over from where he's standing in the woods.

Steve Chapman

For Further Reflection
John 8:47; Luke 8:15

TODAY'S PRAYER

Lord Jesus, in a world of almost constant sound, help me to sift through the noise and hear your truth. And not just to hear it, but to embrace it, even when it's not what I want to hear.

Press On

Forgetting the past...I press on.

PHILIPPIANS 3:13–14

'm sure you've heard it said that we only use about 10 percent of our brains, but that's a myth. We use all of our brains, though that might be hard to believe when you see the foolish choices some people make.

If you've recently crashed spiritually and are battling to overcome shame, one of your biggest challenges is going to be channeling your considerable brain power in the right direction. Very likely you will be tempted to overthink what happened, to look back and analyze (and then reanalyze, and then analyze again) everything you said or did right up to the moment of the crash. It will feel like this is something you should do to make sure the same thing never happens again.

But there is a problem.

After making a terrible mistake, most people who start analyzing what happened don't know when to quit. They go over and over it, beating the proverbial dead horse until they feel like garbage. Often, they end up in despair, hating themselves, and sometimes make a terrible decision as a result.

My advice is to do some reflecting. Take a day or two if you need it and sort through what happened and why. Then stop and move on to the next step, whatever that might be. Perhaps you need to offer an apology to someone or make an adjustment to your lifestyle. Certainly, it will involve spending some time with God. The important thing is to keep moving forward. Don't let yourself get stuck in one place.

If beating yourself up worked, you'd be rich, thin, and happy. Try loving yourself instead.

Cheryl Richardson

For Further Reflection

Hebrews 12:1; James 1:12

TODAY'S PRAYER

Dear Lord, give me eyes to see the futility of continuing to browbeat myself for what I did. Help me to trust the sufficiency of your grace and press on in true repentance.

DAY 49

Don't Assume

Look beneath the surface so you can judge correctly.

JOHN 7:24

One night Jesus' disciples were in a boat crossing the Sea of Galilee. The Bible says the wind was howling and battering their vessel to the point that, even as experienced seamen, they were afraid for their lives. About three o'clock in the morning, Jesus came to them, walking on the water. They saw Jesus' figure in the flashes of lightning and assumed he was a ghost.

Anybody who's read the story in Matthew 14 can sympathize with the disciples' reaction. Assumptions are so easy to make.

We assume the server who is late with our iced tea refill is inattentive, when in fact she is covering extra tables because a coworker went home sick. We assume the person at church who never says hello is rude, when in fact he has anxiety attacks in public places but fights through them to come to church anyway. We assume that a prayer hasn't been answered because we didn't get what we asked for, when in fact God, in his wisdom, granted us a far greater gift and saved us untold problems by vetoing our request.

Are you making some assumptions in the aftermath of your sin?

Are you assuming that God now considers you damaged goods and will never again offer you an opportunity to serve him?

Are you assuming that the people who know about your sin will never respect you again? Don't assume.

Instead, remember that the same Peter who assumed he was about to die in a storm at the hands of a ghost walked on water a few minutes later.

I fail to see Jesus because I am too busy assuming it isn't him.

Grace Valentine

For Further Reflection

Proverbs 18:2; 1 John 4:1

TODAY'S PRAYER

Lord Jesus, you are wonderfully unpredictable. Forgive me for occasionally forgetting this, and arrogantly assuming what you're up to instead of humbly waiting for you to unfold your plan.

Reboot

He has created us anew in Christ Jesus,
so we can do the good things
he planned for us long ago.

EPHESIANS 2:10

Isn't rebooting a wonderful concept? Your device starts acting a little wonky, you get frustrated and don't know what to do, and then it hits you: "Maybe if I just reboot..." So you do and your problem is gone! Computer experts say that rebooting corrects 90% of computer problems.

Rebooting is more than restarting; it's powering your computer down and waiting thirty seconds before you start it up again. That waiting period causes the computer to execute its boot process, which clears away issues and glitches, some of which were likely causing problems.

In a sense, we get to restart our lives every morning when we get out of bed. But restarting is not rebooting. Rebooting is going back to the foundational truths upon which our lives should be built. One of those is in our verse for today. Paul says that we were saved to serve the Lord, to do the good things God has planned for us.

Mark it down. When sin wrecks our lives, it's *always* because we have gotten off track and are serving ourselves first. It's the ultimate life glitch—putting yourself and your desires before God and his desires. Reversing this mindset is the quickest way to bring dramatic change to your messed-up life.

So, this morning when you got out of bed you restarted your life, but did you reboot it? Did you start completely fresh, with serving God as your new priority? Until you do, that same old glitch will continue to make your life miserable.

Knowing that God created me for his exclusive purposes validates my life more than any honor or accolade I achieved as a baseball player.

Darryl Strawberry

For Further Reflection

Romans 8:6; Lamentations 3:22-23

TODAY'S PRAYER

Father, I confess my selfishness. I have cared far too much about what I want and have forgotten that I am here to serve you. Help me reboot my life and start fresh with your will as my priority.

Stay With It

Blessed is the man who remains steadfast under trial.

JAMES 1:12 ESV

Occasionally, someone who has sinned greatly will bemoan the difficulty he is facing, as if some great, unwarranted trial has come into his life. He will hang his head and say, "I'm really going through a hard time," as if to elicit sympathy. The truth is, he is reaping what he has sown. The only reason he is mired in difficulty is because he made a horrendous moral choice.

A single sin can populate our lives with trouble. For example, an affair can crash your marriage, turn your children against you, cost you the respect of your friends, and, if you happen to be in ministry or another line of work where reputation is of supreme importance, cost you your career. Even if you repent quickly and get your life back on track, you'll still be trying to clean up the mess you've made for a long time. It could take months, or even years, to regain the trust of those who feel betrayed by your actions.

Maybe that's where you are now—in the aftermath of your sin. You've repented, but you're not even close to having the mess cleaned up. And maybe the whole process is starting to get you down. You're frustrated that the people who are important to you aren't coming around as quickly as you hoped they would. Your sin wasn't a trial; it was a choice. But now you *are* facing a trial, that of remaining steadfast and patient while things move slowly.

Consider this feeling of frustration and impatience a test of the sincerity of your repentance. If you humbly acknowledge that you and you alone are the cause of this trouble and determine to work through the process of restoration—however long it takes—healing will eventually come. Just stay with it.

When everything seems to be going against you, remember that the airplane takes off against the wind, not with it.

Henry Ford

For Further Reflection

Joshua 1:9; Galatians 5:1

TODAY'S PRAYER

Dear Father, forgive me when I act as though the pain of my sin is an imposition unfairly thrust upon me. Help me patiently work through the process of restoration, however long it takes.

The Lure of Sin

The spirit is willing, but the body is weak.

MATTHEW 26:41

"I could lose weight if I didn't have to drive by the Krispy Kreme every day on my way to work."

"I never would have cheated on my wife if my coworker hadn't come on to me."

"I wasn't online looking for porn, but when that link came up it caught my attention."

One of the keys to succeeding in life is simply to understand how weak and vulnerable you are. There's not a person alive who doesn't have a weak spot—or 10 or 12. Sometimes we are surprised when we hear about a high-profile Christian who has fallen into sin. We shouldn't be. If David, a man after God's own heart, could have an affair and commit what amounted to murder to hang onto his mistress, then anybody can have a moral failure.

There is both encouragement and warning in this truth. The encouragement comes from knowing that if you feel weak and vulnerable, you're not alone. Even the people around you who seem so strong and spiritually invincible are just like you. They have weaknesses too.

The warning should be obvious: You can't let your guard down for even a moment. In fact, Satan is waiting for you to do just that. The Bible tells us that he is looking for someone to devour. Basically, he's looking for someone *easy* to devour, someone with his or her guard down.

If you hope to live the rest of your life without repeating the sin that has caused you shame, you must identify your weaknesses and bolster your defenses. Every hour of every day you must be on guard.

Everything I like is either illegal, immoral, or fattening.

Alexander Wolcott

For Further Reflection
Psalm 73:26; 2 Corinthians 12:9

TODAY'S PRAYER

Father, I am so weak. Like the Apostle Paul, I always seem to end up doing the things I don't want to do. Help me also to be as diligent as he was at pursuing righteousness.

Hallow His Name

Our Father in heaven, may your name be kept holy.

MATTHEW 6:9

Some people are very casual with God's name. And no, I'm not referring to unbelievers who use his name as a curse word. I'm referring to Christians who refer to him as "the man upstairs" or "the big guy in the sky" or some other flippant phrase. Many Christians will use God's name as an exclamation—"Oh my God!"—every time something unexpected happens. And the abbreviation "OMG" is no better.

Why talk about this in a book about overcoming shame? Because the way we view God has a lot to do with the way we respond to his commands. If we treat God flippantly, there's every reason to believe we'll treat his commands the same way.

When Jesus gave us what we now call the Lord's Prayer, he established respect for God's name in the first line. Interestingly, most of us kind of glide over that line when we read and study the prayer. We find more food for thought and discussion in the lines having to do with forgiveness and temptation. Perhaps we should go back to that first line and realize how important it is. In fact, is there anything we do, any choice we make in life, that isn't influenced by how we view God?

Do you hallow God's name, treating it with honor and respect?

If not, you need to start.

He is not a man, and he is not upstairs. He is your Creator, the Almighty God of the universe, and the only hope you have for salvation. Act like it.

There is salvation by no other name. Live as those who are marked by it. Let every other name be forgotten and this one endure. Let every other name sink into darkness and this one shine forth like the noonday sun.

Jen Wilkin

For Further Reflection

Proverbs 18:10; Exodus 20:7

TODAY'S PRAYER

Father in Heaven, in a world that constantly diminishes you, I want to be one who glorifies you. Help me to remember that it all begins with the attitude of my heart and the words that come out of my mouth.

Laugh More

A cheerful heart is good medicine.

Proverbs 17:22

If you're struggling to move forward in the aftermath of a terrible sin, you probably haven't been laughing much. The shame you feel probably takes the humor out of every potentially giggle-worthy moment. Maybe you've wondered if anything will ever seem funny again. Or maybe you would like to laugh, but feel like doing so would trivialize your sin, that a person who's been as bad as you have been has forfeited the right to have fun.

God would disagree. Yes, he would want you to take your sin seriously, but he told us that a cheerful heart is good medicine. And we know from medical science that laughter is good for us. It strengthens the immune system, reduces stress, and burns calories! There's even research to indicate that people who laugh a lot live longer.

You might say, "But after what I did, what do I have to be happy about?"

How about the fact that your sin has been forgiven? How about the fact that, even though you were conquered by temptation, you are more than a conqueror through the blood of Christ? How about the fact that God can take all things—even your sin—and bring good out of it?

Steer clear of people who think you should spend the rest of your life punishing yourself. Yes, you should weep and repent, but whatever you do, don't turn your life into one big pity party. The life of faith presents us with so many reasons to rejoice. And those reasons never go away, even when we have made mistakes.

I believe laughter is like a needle and thread. Deftly used, it can patch up just about everything.

Barbara Johnson

For Further Reflection

Ecclesiastes 3:4; Psalm 126:2

TODAY'S PRAYER

Dear Father, help me to accept the forgiveness
you offer and to find the simple humor
in daily life and to relish the joy
that comes from knowing you.

Repent and Replace

*Prove by the way you live that you have repented
of your sins and turned to God.*

MATTHEW 3:8

Television shows about remodeling old houses are popular, and it's not hard to understand why. Extensive expertise and creativity go into turning an old home into a sparkling new showcase. We like to see how it's done, and maybe file away some ideas to incorporate into our own homes someday.

Every major remodeling job includes "demo day," the day everyone grabs a crowbar or a sledgehammer and starts demolishing. What great therapy! You can take out all your frustrations by destroying things...and not get into trouble for it!

Sometimes things in our lives need to be demolished, such as attitudes and habits and relationships...things that are leading us away from God and into trouble. The sin that brought shame into your life was likely tied to something unhealthy that needed to be demolished, and maybe you've already demolished it. That's generally what we do when sin blows up in our faces. We make a quick, radical change. That's good, but don't think you can relax.

Demo day is only the beginning of the project. Next comes the rebuilding, the shaping of something better. This is the part of overcoming shame that doesn't get enough attention. Everybody is quick to tell you that you need to quit this or that, but they don't give nearly enough attention to the importance of replacing what you're quitting with something better.

What are you building in your life to replace what needed to be torn down? Do you have a new attitude under construction? A new way of managing your time? A new approach to relationships? The key to building a better life is not just to repent, but to repent and replace.

You may clear some plot of land of every noxious weed, but that will not make of it a garden.... It becomes a garden when flowers are growing there.

Charles L. Allen

For Further Reflection
Isaiah 61:4; Luke 15:10

TODAY'S PRAYER

Lord, I know demolition is a part of your plan. Help me to swing the sledgehammer without reservation so that I can make room for new attitudes and habits that will give you the glory you deserve.

DAY 56

Go to Church

Let us not neglect our meeting together,
as some people do.

HEBREWS 10:25

A moral failure often causes a person to drop out of church, and it's understandable. The shame and embarrassment make the thought of facing one's friends and pastor almost unbearable. Some people consider going to a different church where they can relax a little because no one knows them. However, that often doesn't work as well as they think it will. The feeling of worshiping in a different church among strangers only emphasizes the fact that something is terribly wrong.

At that point it's almost inevitable that the person will consider not going to church at all. *I can worship at home... have my own private time with God. I can stream sermons on TV and donate money. I can do everything at home I would do at church.*

Not quite.

In our verse for today you'll see an eight-letter word that is critical to our understanding of the healthy Christian life. It's the word "together." Private worship is fine, but not to the exclusion of worshiping with other people. When we worship with others, we stand a much greater chance of being inspired. Other people's victories remind us of what is possible for us. We also have accountability when we place ourselves under the authority of church leaders. And if

118

you've been waylaid by sin, accountability is probably exactly what you need.

Go to church. If it's painful and embarrassing at first, so be it. Accept the embarrassment as one of the consequences of your sin and move on. People will respect you more than if you run and hide. And then you can begin rebuilding that trust.

It is commonplace to hear people declare that they don't need to unite with a church to be a Christian.... This is not the testimony of the great saints of history; it is the confession of fools.

R. C. Sproul

For Further Reflection

Matthew 18:20; Psalm 122:1

TODAY'S PRAYER

Lord, I need to be reconciled to you, but also to your people. Give me the courage to return to my church family, and help me find the encouragement and accountability I need.

Singular Focus

*If you look for me wholeheartedly,
you will find me.*

JEREMIAH 29:13

You've seen pictures of European cities bombed during World War II, full of rubble, broken-down walls, and roofs with gaping holes. Something similar can happen when a person is caught in sin. The devastation is often widespread, potentially affecting the person's emotions, self-image, relationships, family, church, and career. Many people feel hopeless, wondering how they're ever going to rebuild a life in such shambles.

Maybe that's where you are right now.

If so, understand that although there may be many things in your life that are broken and need to be rebuilt, nothing is more important than seeking the Lord and drawing near to him once more. In fact, until you find God again, you'll never be able to restore the various areas of your life properly. You might offer apologies and patch up some things, but until God is back at the center of your life, nothing is going to be quite right.

Today's verse offers an important word of caution. God says that if you want to find him, you must seek him *wholeheartedly*. In other words, for right now, you need to forget the broken stuff in your life and just seek him. Make him your only priority. The issues you have to address aren't going anywhere. After you've reestablished your relationship with the Lord, you'll be truly ready to tackle the job of rebuilding the devastated areas of your life properly.

The mark of a great man is one who knows when to set aside the important things in order to accomplish the vital ones.

Brandon Sanderson

For Further Reflection

Deuteronomy 10:12; Matthew 6:33

TODAY'S PRAYER

Father in heaven, I need you at the center of my life if I am to recover from the devastation my sin has caused. Help me to seek you wholeheartedly and not get distracted by other concerns.

Blaming God

*People ruin their lives by their own foolishness
and then are angry at the LORD.*

PROVERBS 19:3

The Innocence Project is an organization that fights for the rights of people who have been wrongly accused and convicted of a crime. Since the late 1980s there have been almost 300 DNA exonerations in the United States and over 800 total exonerations, leading experts to believe that about one percent of the prison population (about 20,000 inmates) are falsely convicted.

It would be a terrible thing to be falsely accused and convicted just one time. So imagine how God feels when he is falsely accused and convicted by millions of people day after day. It's very common for people who find themselves in trouble to look at God and say, "Why didn't you protect me? Why didn't you step in and stop me before I went too far? Why didn't you reveal to me that I was making a bad decision?"

No one gets blamed more than God. Try blaming a human who's innocent and that individual will protest. But God will remain silent and let you heap all the blame on him you want. Does he like it? No. But he can handle it.

If you've been blaming God for your troubles, you need to stop. Blaming God for your sin is like blaming your doctor because you smoked for 40 years and got lung cancer.

Imagine yelling at your physician, "You knew smoking was bad for me! Why didn't you stop me?"

There will be no healing or restoration in your life until you make peace with the One who can provide it. It's not complicated. Take responsibility for what you did and humble yourself before the only One who can help you.

We may never understand why God does everything he does, but to question him? To suggest he should have tried just a little bit harder to make things more to our liking? God have mercy on us!

Gary L. Thomas

For Further Reflection

Isaiah 45:9-10; Job 1:22

TODAY'S PRAYER

Gracious Father, I alone am responsible for my choices. I promise to stop looking for ways to take myself off the hook. Please forgive me for the blame I have placed on you and others.

Time

Your life is like the morning fog—
it's here a little while, then it's gone.

JAMES 4:14

There are three great things about time.

One, you have it. You may not have money or influential friends or credentials or a hundred other things that can be beneficial. But you've got time.

Two, time can be apportioned however you want. If you go to school or work, someone else will tell you what to do with some of your time. Otherwise, you're free to decide how much time you want to apply to different priorities. This puts greater power in your hands than you may realize.

Three, time has magical powers. Think about how often you've been stuck in a situation where you didn't know what to do next, so you said, "Let's just give it time." Why would you say that? Because you know time has an uncanny ability to heal, sort out confusion, and cause answers to emerge that seem elusive in the moment.

But here's one more thing about time: it's unforgiving. Its rules do not change. For example, it won't slow down. In a basketball game, you can call time out; in life you can't. Seconds relentlessly tick off the clock. If you waste time, no one is going to say, "Hey, you're a nice guy so I'm going to back up the clock and let you try again."

Why all this talk about time in a book about overcoming shame? Because time will be a friend if you respect it and treat it properly. Your sin may have alienated key people in your life...it may have cost you so much. But time will always work for you if you make good choices. Give it time and ask God to show you steps you can take each day.

If my private world is in order, it is because I have made a daily determination to see time as God's gift and worthy of careful investment.

Gordon MacDonald

For Further Reflection

Ephesians 5:16; John 9:4

TODAY'S PRAYER

Lord, thank you for the time you have given me. I haven't used it as well as I could have in the past, but I commit to using it wisely in the future.

Sit Tight

Be patient in trouble.

Romans 12:12

Yesterday we talked about the value of time. But managing time well does not mean you should always be doing something. There are many moments in life when the best thing you can do is just sit tight.

One such situation is when you're waiting on someone to make a key decision that impacts you. You might be tempted to badger or pressure the person into making the choice you're hoping for. Instead, take a step back and wait.

Another moment is when you've done all you can do and said everything there is to say. You can keep repeating yourself, but you will likely make yourself a nuisance, which won't help your cause. Be patient.

A third circumstance in which it's important to sit tight is when the machinery of life needs time to work. As mentioned in yesterday's devotion, time has magical powers if you'll just let it do its thing. Being antsy or trying to rush things along doesn't help, and may in fact hurt your cause.

If you've apologized and are waiting on someone to forgive you, sit tight.

If you're hurting and wondering when healing will come, sit tight.

If you're hoping for a second chance to come your way, sit tight.

Time might not heal all wounds, but no wound has a chance of healing without time.

How poor are they that have not patience! What wound did ever heal but by degrees?

William Shakespeare

For Further Reflection

Romans 8:25; Romans 12:12

TODAY'S PRAYER

Dear Father, I often feel like I need to do something, even when I've done all I can do. Help me to know when I need to just sit tight and trust you.

Anger Danger

Human anger does not produce the righteousness God desires.

JAMES 1:20

If you have sinned, you know it. You're probably also willing to accept responsibility and face the consequences. But there could be another factor in play that is causing you trouble: the person who helped you sin. Or perhaps tempted you in the beginning. Maybe you had an affair, and honestly feel that if your coworker hadn't started flirting with you, nothing would have happened. Maybe you were dishonest in your job but believe the situation only happened because your boss put unreasonable pressure on you to produce. Maybe you struck someone but feel that you were provoked.

Obviously, anger is the natural response when you feel you've been wronged. And that anger can burn especially hot when the person who wronged you does not appear to be suffering any repercussions while you are being publicly shamed and embarrassed.

It is critical that you not allow your anger to bubble and boil in your gut. First, anger intensifies if it isn't dealt with. When we encounter a person who hasn't addressed his anger, we generally say he has a lot of hostility—he's mad at everything and everybody. Maybe his anger was initially directed at a specific thing but has now infiltrated every corner of his life.

Second, unaddressed anger will keep you from finding restoration and peace. The fact that you're reading this book indicates that you truly want to move past your sin in a healthy, God-honoring way. That can't happen if you choose to nurture your anger. You must forgive the person you feel bears some of the responsibility for what happened. Let God deal with that person. And make no mistake...he will.

Anger is an acid that can do more harm to the vessel in which it is stored than to anything on which it is poured.

Mark Twain

For Further Reflection

Ephesians 4:26; Proverbs 29:11

TODAY'S PRAYER

Gracious Father, you know I sinned, but didn't sin alone. Right now, I entrust to you everything that happened. I release it all to your care and attention. Help me to move on in peace.

Little Foxes

Catch all the foxes, those little foxes,
before they ruin the vineyard of love.

SONG OF SOLOMON 2:15

In Old Testament times, vineyards were big business. They made money for their owners and kept people supplied with grapes and wine. The biggest threat to a vineyard was not weather or thieves, but the little foxes that sneaked in and ate the grapes and destroyed the vines. If you read the Song of Solomon, you realize that the author is referring to the relationship between a man and a woman, and how it's the little things that are apt to ruin it.

You might be facing little foxes as you try to overcome the shame that sin brought into your life. Maybe you've done the big things you needed to do, like confessing and repenting and apologizing to the people you hurt, but the little things are slowing you down.

For example, maybe you're bearing some resentment toward a friend you feel didn't support you during your time of crisis. Maybe you were there for that person when he or she needed a friend, but when *you* were the one in need, the favor was not returned.

Or maybe you finally summoned the courage to go back to church and happened to overhear someone make a gossipy comment about you...someone you thought you could count on for support, not criticism.

These things are typical human behavior. They're disappointing but not surprising. But they can become the raspberry seed in your wisdom tooth, that thing that eats at you and distracts you from your purpose if left unresolved. Let these situations go and move on; you have bigger, more important things to focus on.

Men do not stumble over mountains, but over molehills.

Confucius

For Further Reflection

Luke 16:10; Matthew 13:32

TODAY'S PRAYER

Lord Jesus, in the Gospels I see that you were tolerant and forgiving of so much disappointing behavior. Help me to be the same, so that I can continue to move forward with my life.

When You Lose Respect

Even my own brothers pretend they don't know me;
they treat me like a stranger.

PSALM 69:8

Fifty years ago, Rodney Dangerfield was one of the most popular comedians in America. He presented himself as a nervous, uptight guy who just couldn't catch a break. He would tug on his tie and wipe sweat off his face as he explained his misery. The line that made him famous was, "I tell you, I get no respect." And then he would explain how everyone from his wife to the family dog disrespected him.

Rodney Dangerfield was wildly popular because everyone knew he was joking. If people had thought for a moment that he really was constantly disrespected, they wouldn't have laughed because being disrespected for real is not funny.

Have you felt the pain of disrespect in the aftermath of your sin? Are people in your workplace whispering behind your back while giving you the cold shoulder? Are people you used to hang out with no longer including you, or now always busy when you call? Does that person you've had problems with in the past now act infuriatingly smug when you're around?

Jeremiah was a prophet who felt the sting of disrespect. At one point he wrote, "My own people laugh at me. All day long they sing their mocking songs," (Lamentations 3:14). However, just nine verses later he wrote, "The faithful love of the Lord never ends! His mercies never cease," (Lamentations 3:22).

Jeremiah understood what you must understand, that for a season, you may have to live with the "mocking songs" of unkind people, but God's mercy will be sufficient to keep you going until you can win back their respect. And even if some people never again respect you, it's okay. It's not in them that your future health and happiness will be found anyway. It's in God.

The glory of God's faithfulness is that no sin of ours has ever made him unfaithful.

Charles Spurgeon

For Further Reflection

Romans 12:12; 1 Peter 3:9

TODAY'S PRAYER

Father, I know that some people will not respond to my sin in a loving way. Help me to forgive them and to always look to you for the love and grace I need.

Yes and No

Just say a simple, "Yes, I will," or "No, I won't."

MATTHEW 5:37

M otivational experts are big on saying yes. *Yes* is positive. It sets people in motion (which motivational experts love), while *no* keeps people in place and digs in their heels (which motivational experts hate). But the Bible stresses the importance of saying both yes *and* no.

After Jesus was baptized, Satan tempted him three times. Jesus said, "No, I won't" to every one of those temptations. Later, when he faced the crucifixion, he could have decided not to go through with it. But he said, "Yes, I will" and paid the price for our sins.

The key is knowing when to say yes and when to say no. It's not always easy.

Maybe you've had someone in your life for a long time, but the relationship has turned toxic and is hindering your spiritual growth. You will likely feel obligated to say yes to continuing that relationship because of the history you share. But you really should say no for the sake of your spiritual health.

Or maybe your job is putting you in an environment that is hindering your comeback. The idea of starting over in a new job and maybe taking a pay cut makes you want to say no to leaving where you are. But until you say yes to a new path forward, you're likely going to find real progress hard to come by.

There is no one-size-fits-all answer to life's questions. Sometimes yes is the right answer. But don't let the motivational experts fool you into believing no isn't a good answer. Sometimes stubborn, dug-in heels are exactly what the situation calls for.

The difference between perseverance and obstinacy is that one comes from a strong will and the other comes from a strong won't.

Henry Ward Beecher

For Further Reflection

Leviticus 10:10; Proverbs 18:21

TODAY'S PRAYER

Father, it's obvious that I have said yes when I should have said no, and no when I should have said yes. Give me wisdom that I might see more clearly when to say yes or no.

Keep Your Cool

A gentle answer deflects anger,
but harsh words make tempers flare.

PROVERBS 15:1

Here we have a verse that is the favorite of preachers in a generation where so many people seem so very angry. Road rage, Black Friday fisticuffs, screaming at school board meetings, political protests turned violent—there seems to be no end of people blowing their tops. So spiritual leaders point to this verse and encourage people to calm down and use gentle language.

As a person who has sinned, you can count on someone hitting you with some harsh words sooner or later. There will always be a judgmental person who feels the need to put you in your place. It might be someone who suffered because of your sin, which would make them even more irate. Or it might be someone close to the person you sinned against who feels the need to rally around his or her friend.

Unfortunately, they might lash out at you more than once. Depending on the severity of the sin you committed, it's possible that this person will feel the need to attack you whenever your paths cross. If you live in a small town, this could spell trouble.

Here are two suggestions.

First, see the situation as part of the consequences of your sin and accept it humbly. Remember, it's what you did that provoked the person. Let the situation teach you the importance of not making a similar mistake ever again.

Second, steer clear. Even if you have to shop at a different store or quit going to Little League games or even attend a different church for a while, it would certainly be worth it if you could avoid repeated embarrassing confrontations that only add to your stress.

How many times are you going to let people get your goat before you start locking your goat up in a different place?

Levi Lusko

For Further Reflection

Proverbs 25:28; Proverbs 16:32

TODAY'S PRAYER

Lord Jesus, I see in the Gospels how you repeatedly kept your cool when people attacked you, and even betrayed you. Help me to have that same spirit of gentleness every day.

Housecleaning

Let us strip off every weight that slows us down.

HEBREWS 12:1

Spring is a popular time for major housecleaning. When the winter weather breaks and the first warm breezes start to blow, people feel compelled to vacuum, scrub, and dig into their closets and garages and start purging. Drive through the typical subdivision on a warm spring Saturday and you're likely to see piles of junk at the curb, waiting for the garbage truck.

Sin is an indicator of many things, including the presence of something in your life that has become an encumbrance and needs to be gotten rid of. Call it spiritual housecleaning. Maybe the sin that pulled you down is linked to a relationship, job, hobby, routine, or the internet. You must identify what contributed to your sin and make sure that thing is either removed from your life or fitted with restraints that will keep you from misusing it again.

This is likely to be very difficult. You know that the thing in question is a detriment to you, but you love it and don't want to let it go. You'll be likely to look around and point to other people who enjoy the same thing as a way of justifying hanging onto it. But what is a problem for one person might not be a problem for another. It's critical that you identify the stumbling block or hindrance in your life and then address it—even if it takes drastic measures.

Anything we think we need or cannot go without, apart from an intimate relationship with Him, is an idol.

Mo Aiken

For Further Reflection

1 John 2:15; John 12:25

TODAY'S PRAYER

Father in heaven, help me not to love the things of this world. Give me eyes to see the things I need to remove from my life, and the courage to do it and not look back.

The Devil's Favorite Day

*Don't brag about tomorrow, since you don't know
what the day will bring.*

PROVERBS 27:1

There's an old adage claiming that "Tomorrow is Satan's favorite day." The idea is that Satan always—ALWAYS—encourages us to put off doing the things we need to do. He is forever tempting us to wait until tomorrow when we have something important to do. Tomorrow is the day he holds out as a better day than this one to do the right thing.

In contrast, Proverbs 27:1 reminds us that the future—even tomorrow—is uncertain. We don't know what's even 24 hours ahead. Think of today as the Lord's favorite day. Psalm 118:24 says, "This is the day the Lord has made. We will rejoice and be glad in it."

- Do you need to apologize to somebody?
- Do you need to cut ties with somebody who's a negative influence?
- Do you need to recommit to spiritual disciplines, such as prayer and Bible study?
- Do you need to start spending more time with your family?
- Do you need to recommit to your marriage?

If so, Satan will encourage you to wait until tomorrow. He'll supply you with all kinds of reasons why now isn't the best time for you to make changes: *You're working a lot of overtime.*

You probably need to wait until things slow down before you start your daily devotions. He's been in a bad mood—you better wait to have that talk with him. The guys are going golfing today; I'll do something with the kids next *weekend.*

In your fight to overcome shame and put your life back on track, today is the day that really matters.

Satan does not care how spiritual your intentions are, or how holy your resolutions, if only they are determined to be done tomorrow.

J. C. Ryle

For Further Reflection

Romans 13:11; John 4:35

TODAY'S PRAYER

Father, awaken me to the dangers of procrastination and give me a sense of urgency about my spiritual life. Convict me when I get lazy and start making excuses for not moving forward.

Famine

At that time a severe famine struck the land of Canaan, forcing Abram to go down to Egypt, where he lived as a foreigner.

GENESIS 12:10

The Bible tells about many famines, stretches of time when there was no rain and therefore no crops. Some famines lasted years and killed many people. As you read about the famines in Scripture you will notice something interesting: God's people got caught right in the middle of them and suffered like everyone else. Abraham, Isaac, Joseph, Naomi, David, and Elisha all experienced times of famine.

Another thing you'll notice about the famines of the Bible is that many times they were instigated by God as punishment for people's sin. In 2 Kings 8:1-2, the prophet Elisha said to the woman from Shunem, "Take your family and move to some other place, for the Lord has called for a famine on Israel that will last for seven years." We recognize God as the Lord of the feast and praise him when times are good and food is bountiful. But make no mistake, he is also the Lord of the famine.

Metaphorically speaking, you may be in a time of famine right now. Maybe the shortages in your life are draining you—shortages of hope, support, encouragement, energy, and joy. Perhaps your sin and its ramifications have brought you to a desolate place and you feel like giving up.

Don't.

The famine in your life is serving a purpose. It's teaching you the importance of making better choices. It's showing you the futility of sin. It's reminding you that blessedness and bounty come from obedience. Don't run from your famine, learn from it.

Good days. Bad days. God is in *all* days. He is the Lord of the famine and the feast, and he uses both to accomplish his will.

Max Lucado

For Further Reflection

Psalm 73:26; Psalm 27:5

TODAY'S PRAYER

Mighty God, I bow before you as the ruler
of all things, of feasts and famines.
Help me to learn from times of scarcity,
and to trust you to bring me through.

When Much Becomes Little

*"There's a young boy here with five barley loaves
and two fish. But what good is that
with this huge crowd?"*

JOHN 6:9

Put yourself in the shoes of the boy who left his house that day to go hear Jesus teach. He knew he wouldn't be home in time for dinner, so he packed some food. It appears the little guy had quite an appetite because he took five loaves of bread. Even if they weren't as large as the standard loaf of Sara Lee you might find at your local supermarket, five loaves still seems like a lot. And he had two fish, to boot. I don't imagine he had any worries about going hungry that day.

But then suddenly someone was asking for his lunch. A man he didn't know was saying, "Hey, kid, a lot of people are hungry, how about contributing your lunch to the cause?" Just that quickly, what seemed like plenty of food, seemed next to nothing. In a blink, much became little.

Maybe you're having a similar feeling right now. There was a time when it seemed like you had plenty to offer the Kingdom. You had clear talents and abilities that everybody recognized. Maybe you were in ministry or heavily involved in your church. But when sin came into your life, that giftedness and potential seemed to shrink to nothing. Now, in the aftermath of your sin, with shame and embarrassment torturing you, it might seem like you have next to nothing to offer.

Remember the boy with the loaves and fishes. He had a lot, then suddenly what he had seemed like a drop in the bucket...but it didn't matter to Jesus. It's not what you bring to the table, but what *he* brings to the table that makes the difference.

God is great not just because nothing is too big for him; God is also great because nothing is too small.

Mark Batterson

For Further Reflection

Exodus 4:2; Galatians 5:9

TODAY'S PRAYER

Lord, I praise you for your ability to take my meager gifts and use them. Help me never to think that what I have to offer is of no use to you.

Truly Free

If the Son sets you free, you are truly free.

JOHN 8:36

E arly in John 8, Jesus encounters a woman who had been caught in the act of adultery. The Pharisees dragged her before Christ and threw her at his feet. By law, she should have been stoned, but the Pharisees wanted to see if Jesus had the courage to condemn her to death and endanger his reputation as a kind and gracious rabbi. You'll remember that Jesus outsmarted them be saying the person without sin should cast the first stone.

But the best part of the story comes at the very end.

After the Pharisees have wandered off, mumbling their frustration at being thwarted, Jesus is left standing face to face with the young woman. "Where are your accusers?" Jesus asks. "Didn't even one of them condemn you?"

The woman simply says, "No, Lord."

This is the moment when Jesus could have said, "Look, we need to have a little talk. I want to impress upon you the futility of the lifestyle you've been living." For the next 30 minutes, Jesus could have lectured this woman and concluded by saying, "I want you to report back to me in two weeks and we'll talk about what kind of progress you've made." He could have put her on a kind of probation.

But he didn't do that. Instead, he said, "Neither do I condemn you. Go and sin no more."

Simply put, he set her free.

If you have sought forgiveness on God's terms, he's set you free too. Don't make the mistake of continuing to hang on to the junk in your past. When you do that, you forfeit the freedom he grants you and choose to remain in slavery.

You can't be 99 percent free and call that freedom. You can't hold on to even 1 percent of the past and say your chains are broken. Freedom must be complete in order to be called freedom.

Jordan Lee Dooley

For Further Reflection

1 Peter 2:16; 2 Corinthians 3:17

TODAY'S PRAYER

Gracious heavenly father, my past pains me more than words can say. Help me to let it go and move on secure in the knowledge that I am truly, completely forgiven.

Expectations

The hopes of the godly result in happiness, but the expectations of the wicked come to nothing.

PROVERBS 10:28

Everyone has expectations, every minute of every day. When you get up in the morning you might be anticipating a normal day ahead, or a hard day depending on your plans. When you choose a restaurant, you predict a certain experience. When you decide to propose to your sweetheart, it's because you project that the two of you will have a wonderful marriage.

But expectations can change.

And sometimes they need to.

That young couple walking down the aisle might have an unrealistic outlook on marriage. Check in with them a year later and you will likely find that they have lowered the bar to a more realistic level.

Because of your sin, your high hopes might have taken a beating. Maybe your transgression has damaged your reputation or your marriage or even cost you your job. If so, people are going to look at—and perhaps relate to—you differently. Someone you once were close to might not trust you anymore. Someone who used to have so much confidence in you might have all kinds of doubts now.

Don't be angry at these people. Remember, by sinning you put them in the position of having to recalculate their relationship with you. Perhaps someday you can regain their trust and get things back close to the way they were. That should definitely be your goal. But for now, adjust your expectations.

Sometimes our expectations are outdated. They made sense in another season of our lives, but not today.

Valorie Burton

For Further Reflection

Luke 3:15; Luke 12:40

TODAY'S PRAYER

Dear Lord, I want to be as gracious with others as I want them to be with me. Help me to use their doubts about me as fuel to work hard and regain their trust.

Collateral Benefit

Many will see what he has done and be amazed.
They will put their trust in the Lord.

PSALM 40:3

When war breaks out, we often hear the term "collateral damage." It refers to unintended damage that happens as a result of the main action being carried out. A missile, for example, might be intended to take out a terrorist stronghold, but innocent women and children might be there too. Collateral damage is a terrible thing.

There's also such a thing as collateral benefit. When something good happens, people nearby might be blessed by it. It's been said that when a hard-drinking man gets sober, everyone in the household, including the family dog, is happy about it.

Your sin likely caused collateral damage. People close to you were hurt and disappointed, maybe even crushed emotionally. It's possible that your sin did deep damage to a marriage, to innocent children, or to people who had invested in you. This can be a devastating thing to try to work through. One thing that will help is remembering that your repentance and restoration can produce collateral benefit. It won't undo what happened, but it will help bring healing. People will see the change in you. They will recognize that things are different now, that God is working in your life, and it will be a good thing.

Even so, you must not expect too much from the people who've been hurt. It's difficult to bounce back when your world has been rocked to its foundation. But as God continues to work in your life and you continue to change, people will notice and be forced to work this new reality into their calculations.

What God does in you isn't just for you.

Jennie Lusko

For Further Reflection

Matthew 5:16; 1 Peter 3:1

TODAY'S PRAYER

Father, I know I can never undo my sin, but help me to live in such a way that people will see you at work in my life and be encouraged.

Read Them Again, Slowly

God can be trusted to keep his promise.

HEBREWS 10:23

When you've been devastated by sin, God's promises are your lifeline. Most other things in your life have either been damaged or greatly reduced in importance because of the enormity of the trouble you're in. God's promises provide hope and encouragement when those sentiments are in short supply.

For instance, Romans 8:28 says, "And we know that God causes everything to work together for the good of those who love God and are called according to his purpose for them." When you're dealing with the devastating aftermath of your sin or a cataclysmic crack in your integrity, those words can make it possible for you to keep putting one foot in front of the other.

But sometimes the promises we have in our heads are not exactly the promises God made. Be careful not to read something into that verse that isn't there. Notice, it doesn't say that God will cause everything to work together for good *quickly.*

Many people become frustrated with God because he seems to be dragging his feet. They point to Romans 8:28 and say, "Why isn't God doing something? He promised he would work things out for good, but it isn't happening. There's been no healing and nothing good is happening at all."

Be patient. God knows what he's doing.

It's imperative that you read his promises carefully, especially when you think he seems to be breaking one. He's going to act on what he said, not on what you think he said.

Sometimes we find ourselves frustrated with God because we have believed him for a promise based in the Scriptures to be fulfilled that he never gave us.

Nicki Koziarz

For Further Reflection

Romans 4:20–21; Joshua 21:45

TODAY'S PRAYER

Father, I love your promises and the hope
they give me. Help me to read them carefully
and to trust you for what they say,
and not for what I might want them to say.

Listening vs. Hearing

Whoever has ears, let them hear.

MATTHEW 11:15 NIV

There is a true story about a man who fell asleep during the pastor's sermon. He was sitting in the front row, his head was lolled to one side, and he was breathing deeply and rather noisily. Everyone noticed, especially when the pastor asked the congregation to stand for the final song. You see, the sleeping man was the worship leader! The pastor stretched and stretched and stretched his closing comments until he finally gave up and asked someone sitting near the man to wake him up.

What troubles most pastors is not the occasional person who nods off in church, but the masses of people who sit there wide awake and don't hear a word that's said. I would guess that every Christian who is struggling with shame will admit to having listened to sermons on the sin they committed, perhaps lots of them. Sermons that were likely well-crafted and presented. But listening and hearing are two different things. When you listen to a sermon, the words get inside your ears; when you hear a sermon, the truths get inside your heart.

Think back to the time before you committed the sin that has caused your shame. Were there things being said to you that you didn't hear? Perhaps, a friend, family member, or even a pastor or coach tried to caution you about some of your choices. If so, I suspect you nodded and gave the appearance of hearing, when you were really only listening.

As you work to overcome the shame you feel, you will be trying to improve and get better in several areas of your life. Let how you process truth be one of them. When you're in church, don't just listen to the sermon, hear it. When a friend or family member tries to talk to you about something they see that is concerning, don't just listen, hear. You might not like what you hear, but it could be exactly what you need.

What people fail to learn from sermons they later learn from experience.

Vern McLellan

For Further Reflection
Luke 8:15; John 10:27

TODAY'S PRAYER

Dear Lord, forgive me for those times I have allowed wise words to go in one ear and out the other. Help me in the future not just to open my ears, but to open my heart.

Fences

I looked for someone who might rebuild the wall
of righteousness that guards the land.

EZEKIEL 22:30

In 1934, legendary composer Cole Porter bought a poem from Bob Fletcher, who worked in the Department of Highways in Montana, for $250. He played around with the wording of the poem and put music to it, creating what was later voted one of the top 100 western songs of all time: "Don't Fence Me In." It's a bouncy little song that declares love for the great outdoors and the freedom to do as one pleases.

Fences are often viewed with disdain because they keep us hemmed in. But the greater value of a fence is to keep trouble out. In Bible times, many cities were enclosed by a wall, and nobody screamed, "Don't fence me in!" People in that period knew that a wall or fence could prevent enemy armies from successfully attacking.

Does your life need a fence?

Are battling shame because your enemy, Satan, was able to infiltrate? Did he sneak in with a deadly temptation and catch you off guard? If so, ask yourself what you could have done to protect yourself. Would better time management have made a good fence? How about wiser choices about friendships? Or better discretion in what you read or watch on TV?

We live in a time when people rail against anything that feels restricting, but it is no coincidence that people who demand a "fence-free life" often suffer in ways that people with well-fortified lives do not. If you want to keep from repeating the sin that brought you shame, a fence might be a good idea.

Fences communicate your belief that your land holds life worthy of safeguarding.

Jennifer Dukes Lee

For Further Reflection

Proverbs 14:16; Proverbs 22:3

TODAY'S PRAYER

Dear Father, thank you for the commands you've given that help protect me. When I feel restricted, help me realize that your laws are the secret to my safety and happiness.

Excuses

But they all began making excuses.

Luke 14:18

The Reader's Digest carried a list of some of the funniest (or most ridiculous) excuses people gave for not being able to go to work. One said he mistakenly ate a can of cat food instead of tuna and became deathly sick. Another said he got stuck in the blood pressure machine at the grocery store and couldn't get out. Yet another said he was driving down the road when his false teeth suddenly flew out the window. No word on whether they were in his mouth at the time.

We laugh at excuses like this, but excuse-making is really quite dangerous. People who make excuses are trying to absolve themselves from responsibility for their mistakes, but what they're actually doing is ensuring that their bad behavior and the trouble connected to it will continue. No one has ever become a better person by shifting blame to others or making up flimsy justifications for failures.

People who help celebrities and politicians with damage control when they say or do something stupid always recommend that they own their mistakes. They know it's better to take the heat and get it over with than try to wiggle out of trouble with excuses that keep the social media crowd boiling with anger for weeks or months.

But as a Christian, you have an even better reason not to make excuses: they keep you from being right with God. Our promise of forgiveness hinges on our willingness to admit and confess our sins. Listen to yourself as you talk about the sin that brought you shame. Have excuses started creeping into your explanations? Have you become philosophical about it as time has passed? If so, stop it. Own your sin and trust God's forgiveness.

As regards my own sins it is a safe bet (though not a certainty) that the excuses are not really as good as I think.

C. S. Lewis

For Further Reflection

Genesis 3:13; Proverbs 19:5

TODAY'S PRAYER

Heavenly Father, forgive me for those times I have tried to mitigate my guilt with excuses. Help me to be honest with myself and with you, and to trust your forgiveness.

Be You

How precious are your thoughts about me, O God.

PSALM 139:17

S ocial media is practically built on a very human desire to imitate. Popular looks, destinations, experiences, and even attitudes spread quickly. Look at viral fads on YouTube or TikTok, where everyone posts videos of the same dance move or challenge. Consider the world of comedy and impressions, when a whole career is built of off mimicry, and we are entertained by it. And what about movies? Hardly a month goes by without yet another superhero movie being released!

These are fun and lighthearted forms of imitation. But some forms of mimicry can get you in trouble. Many teenagers try to mirror the behavior of the popular kids out of a desire to be accepted, even to the point of doing things they know are wrong. Many adults have overspent on a home, vehicle, or gadgets in an effort to be socially accepted. Perhaps the sin that is now causing you shame was at least partially the result of you trying to be someone or something different from who you really are.

Sometimes it's good to take some time and think about who you are. God gave you a unique mind and personality. He gave you a one-of-a-kind set of talents and abilities. He gave you aptitudes and passions. It would be a terrible shame if you sacrificed all that specialness to try to be like someone else. Today's verse reminds us that God knows us as individuals. He thinks about you—the special, unique you that he crafted in your mother's womb. Don't disappoint him by discarding that person and trying to be someone else.

Be yourself; everyone else is already taken.

Oscar Wilde

For Further Reflection

Jeremiah 1:5; 1 Corinthians 14:7

TODAY'S PRAYER

My God and Creator, thank you for making me special and unique. Help me to embrace and develop the gifts you've given me and not to worry about or chase the ones you haven't.

You're Not a Superhero

He knows how weak we are;
he remembers we are only dust.

PSALM 103:14

There's a humorous story about Muhammad Ali when he was the reigning heavyweight champ. He boarded a 747 for a commercial flight and took his seat in the first-class section of the plane. When the aircraft was ready to take off, the flight attendant passed by for her final check and asked the champ to fasten his seatbelt. Ali said, "Superman don't need no seatbelt." To which the flight attendant replied, "Superman don't need no plane."

One of the keys to your success as you move forward is to remember that you are not a superhero. You might think you can be a good Christian without giving attention to the spiritual disciplines, but you can't. You might think you can manage your life just fine on your own wisdom, but you can't. You might think you can stay on the straight and narrow without someone to hold you accountable, but you can't. You might think you can skate close to the edge of morality without veering over the line, but you can't.

Psalm 103:14 reminds us that when God made man, he made him out of dust. Not out of steel or concrete or solid rock, but out of dust. What is flimsier than dust? A puff of air disperses it.

But there's no disgrace in being what God made you. There's no disgrace in having weakness. God has made his power available to us through the Holy Spirit, so our weakness does not have to spell our doom. The problem arises when we aren't willing to admit that we're made of dust...when we think we're superheroes. To paraphrase the Apostle Paul in 1 Corinthians 10:12, beware when you think you can fly, lest you crash.

When God is our strength, it is strength indeed; when our strength is our own, it is only weakness.

Saint Augustine

For Further Reflection

Hebrews 4:15; 1 Chronicles 16:11

TODAY'S PRAYER

Lord Jesus, when I get cocky, humble me.
Remind me that I am made of dust
and that I need you in my life every day
to keep from crashing.

Lasting Influence

Let your good deeds shine out for all to see, so that everyone will praise your heavenly Father.

MATTHEW 5:16

In Steve Farrar's book *Finishing Strong*, he asks readers to imagine stepping into a time machine and going back to the first century to ask people a simple question: "Two thousand years from now, who you do think people will remember from your generation?" He supposes that people would answer, "Why, Caesar and Nero, of course!"

How many people do you know named Caesar or Nero?

On the other hand, how many people do you know named Peter or Paul?

Steve makes the point that the key to building a life of lasting influence is not to grab as much power as possible, but to humble yourself and honor God. Being morally perfect is not a prerequisite for lasting influence either. Both Peter and Paul sinned grievously, yet we love and respect them because they did not allow their bad choices to define them.

This is great news as you think about where you go from here. Of course, you want to follow a straight path and not repeat your bad choices. But you can aim higher. You can be a great influence on others, not by working your way into some powerful position but simply by living a life that shines light in the darkness. That's what Peter and Paul did. And Mary and Martha. And Barnabas and Silas. And...well, you get the idea. These people from the Bible whom we have so much respect for and who influence the way we live were ordinary people who honored God.

A life is not important except in the impact it has on other lives.

Jackie Robinson

For Further Reflection
Proverbs 27:17; 1 Peter 2:12

TODAY'S PRAYER

Father, I want to be a light in the darkness. Help me to learn from my mistakes and choose a path forward that is going to help shine more brightly than I ever have.

Who's Got Your Ear?

Fools think their own way is right.

PROVERBS 12:15

There's good news and bad news if you have fallen into sin and are battling shame. The good news is, you're not alone. Everyone has sinned and fallen short of the glory of God. Maybe they've gotten caught and maybe they haven't. Maybe they admit their sin or maybe they don't. But don't be fooled: every person you meet is just as much a sinner as you are.

The bad news is that you will encounter a lot of people who, knowing your sin, will want to impart their wisdom to you. Notice I said *their* wisdom. Not God's, theirs. For some reason people think that experiencing something one time makes them an expert. "I've been through what you're going through, so I know from experience what you need to do."

There was an older woman who overheard a couple of young women at church talking about marriage. The older woman inserted herself into the conversation by saying, "I've been married five times. If anybody is an expert in marriage, it's me." The young women were polite enough not to say it, but later they agreed that the woman was no expert at all, having tried five times and failing every time!

As you seek to put your life back together and overcome shame, it's imperative that you be careful who you listen to. In fact, be particularly wary of anybody who seeks you out and seems determined to advise you. Even if they say they've been down the same road you're traveling, that doesn't mean they traveled it well. Experience doesn't necessarily equal expertise. You'll be wise to seek your counsel from the Word of God. Beyond that, only listen to someone you know well and trust.

Never trust anyone completely but God. Love people, but put your full trust only in God.

Lawrence Welk

For Further Reflection

Proverbs 1:7; Proverbs 13:20

TODAY'S PRAYER

Lord, give me the wisdom I need to weed out those voices I shouldn't be listening to. At the same time, help me to make your Word the lamp unto my feet you've promised it is.

What's Your Weakness?

*Keep watch and pray, so that you will not
give in to temptation.*

MATTHEW 26:41

All professional sports depend on scouting, especially
baseball. Every move a player makes on the field is
charted. Every pitch he faces is noted, along with how that
pitch impacted the game. Consequently, there is a "book" on
every player, a scouting report that tells the opposition what
pitches a player can hit and which ones he can't. If the player
has a specific weakness, opposing pitchers will be aware of
that weakness and use it to their own advantage, repeatedly.

Satan is the same way. He has a book on you, a detailed
scouting report. He knows what your weaknesses are—and
he'll go after them again and again. We all know people
who tend to make the same mistakes: the person who *always*
has financial problems, the person who seems to get let go
from *every* job, the person who can *never* seem to make a
relationship work, the person who is *always* in a dispute with
a neighbor or a co-worker.

Satan knows what every person's weak pitch is, and he just
keeps throwing it. So, what's the solution? Learn to hit that
pitch. Or, spiritually speaking, show Satan that that old trick
won't work on you anymore.

This will be your challenge as you move on from the sin that
brought you shame. Satan knows the temptation he served
up that took you down. He has noted your failure in your

scouting report. You can be sure you will see that temptation again. Your challenge is to prepare yourself for that moment and be ready.

Satan is one of the most unoriginal creatures in the universe. His methods have been effective since the beginning of time. Why change?

Robert Jeffress

For Further Reflection

1 Corinthians 10:13; Ephesians 6:11

TODAY'S PRAYER

Father, my failure has taught me to take my weaknesses seriously. Help me in my efforts to grow stronger, especially in those areas where Satan knows I am weak.

Your Lot in Life

Do everything without complaining.

PHILIPPIANS 2:14

Think about the sin you committed that now has you battling to overcome shame. Do you ever wonder how many other people have committed the same sin—or are committing it right this minute—who have never gotten caught or suffered the consequences you have? God allowed your sin to come to light and, as a result, your life will never be the same, while those other people get to continue, seemingly without repercussions. Maybe someday they will repent and get themselves straightened out without ever having to endure the shame and embarrassment you've had to deal with.

Do you ever ask, "Why me, Lord? Why didn't you give me more time to get my act together?" Or maybe this is the question that gnaws at your gut: "Why did you bring me down, Lord, and not all those other people who are just as guilty?"

Such heavy questions have no answers in this life, so we aren't going to spend any time on them. However, they do bring up the issue of your lot in life. For whatever reason, God either exposed your sin or allowed it to be exposed, and now you're dealing with the aftermath. This is your lot, your reality. You may hate it. The seeming unfairness of it may boil in your gut, but you can't change it. You sinned and there are consequences, now or later. You don't get to choose. God, who chastens his children, does.

This is a tremendous test of your faith and character. To move forward with a sour, complaining spirit will block your healing and restoration. Stop comparing yourself to others and narrow your focus until the only two things you can see are yourself and God. This is between you and him. Nothing else matters.

The important thing about your lot in life is whether you use it for building or parking.

Lee Ezell

For Further Reflection

1 Thessalonians 5:18; Philippians 4:4

TODAY'S PRAYER

Lord, I acknowledge my sin and accept the consequences. Help me to trust your plan for me, even when I see that it differs from your plans for someone else.

Timetables

Hasty shortcuts lead to poverty.

PROVERBS 21:5

Everything we do in life takes *time*. Nothing is instant; even the things we think are instant had lots of time put into them. And some things take a *long* time. For example, it takes:

 ~ Nine months to have a baby.

 ~ Four weeks to get a passport.

 ~ Three days to get to the moon.

 ~ Eighteen months to build a cruise ship.

Right now, the question on your mind is probably, "How long before I'm healed and restored and spiritually healthy again? When can I put the whole sordid episode behind me?"

Of course, the event will always exist in your past as a reminder of what you must not let happen ever again. But when can you expect life to get back to normal?

No one can say for sure.

But don't try to hurry your recovery. The mistake many people make when they have been devastated by sin is to rush through the restoration process. We know eyes are on us. We know people are talking about us and wondering what happened. There's always a morbid curiosity about the sordid details, and so it's only natural to want to charge full steam toward healing and get there as quickly as possible.

But be careful!

You can't recover from major surgery overnight, just as you can't recover from a major moral collapse overnight. A habit may need to be broken. A relationship may need to be restored. A lifestyle may need to be completely changed. These things take time—more time than you want, and likely more time than you think.

You can't expect to overnight break a bad habit you've spent years behaving yourself into.

Andy Stanley

For Further Reflection
Exodus 14:14; Proverbs 19:2

TODAY'S PRAYER

Dear Father, slow me down.
Help me to resist the temptation to fake progress just so I can get through the process faster. Lead me to true healing, even if it means taking the long way around.

The Little Things

It is the smallest of all seeds, but it becomes the largest of garden plants; it grows into a tree, and birds come and make nests in its branches.

MATTHEW 13:32

Most cars that break down don't need a new engine; they need a simple repair.

Most people who feel sick don't need major surgery; they need medicine.

Most students who make bad grades don't need a new school or teacher; they need to study more.

Most married people who are unhappy don't need a new spouse; they need to make an adjustment or two to their relationship.

Fortunately, when things go wrong in life, oftentimes the answer is simple and straightforward—which underscores the importance of the little things.

Take your sin, for example. It may well have caused a great upheaval. It may have cost you some things that are precious to you. It may have hurt people you love. But there's a good chance the cause—and therefore the fix—is rather small. Some of the most common "small" fixes for our "big" problems are:

    ∾ Better time management.

    ∾ More discipline with money.

- ∼ Controlling what we watch and read.
- ∼ Choosing better friends.

I'm not suggesting that these things are always easy. But let's face it: they're not exactly major surgery either. Most people can build a much better life for themselves just by making some simple adjustments.

God is just as interested in your yielding to him in your eating choices and television-watching habits as he is in your choice of a career and spouse.

Lina Abujamra

For Further Reflection

Matthew 25:23; Matthew 3:8

TODAY'S PRAYER

Father, I have not always given enough attention to the little things in my life. Forgive me, and help me as I move forward to be more attentive.

Winning and Losing

Run to win!

1 Corinthians 9:24

The world places a premium on winning. Tom Brady is a legend, not because he's the biggest, strongest, or most agile athlete in professional sports. In fact, every time he plays in a big game the announcers talk about his biggest weakness—the fact that he is not mobile in the pocket. He depends on his offensive linemen to keep the pass rushers away so he has time to throw. But even with that considerable weakness, Brady is universally recognized as the GOAT, the Greatest of All Time, because he has won more Super Bowls than any other quarterback.

Right now, you're probably not feeling much like a winner. Standing in the smoking rubble of your former life, you might feel like the very definition of a loser. But feelings can be deceiving. In God's eyes you're not a winner or loser based on your mistakes but on what you do about your mistakes.

Think about the great heroes of the Bible. All of them had embarrassing moments. All of them did things that would make their mothers blush, and some did things that would get them thrown in jail today. But we still see them as winners because of what they did *after* they sinned. Don't judge yourself by what you've done, because that's not the end of the story. It's always a mistake to jump to conclusions before the story is completely written.

If you learn from defeat, you haven't really lost.

Zig Ziglar

For Further Reflection

2 Timothy 2:5; 2 Timothy 4:7

TODAY'S PRAYER

Father in heaven, I feel like a loser, but I believe
by faith that you simply see me as human.
Help me to learn from my mistakes
and run the rest of my life to win.

This Day

This is the day the LORD has made.

PSALM 118:24

There's a day we are in love with more than any other. We dream about it more than any other. We talk about it more than any other. That day is Someday. Someday is easy to love because it holds any aspiration you have. If you say you're going to be a millionaire by next week, people will express skepticism. But if you say, "Someday I'm going to be a millionaire," no one can really argue with you. Someday can accommodate even our most outlandish dreams. Who doesn't love Someday?

Sometimes because of our love for Someday we fail to make This Day count for all it's worth. When there's work to be done or problems to be dealt with, it's so easy to say, "I'll get around to that Someday." How many people are fully aware they need to deal with some problem in their lives but keep putting it off?

As you continue your journey to overcome shame and build a better life, quit thinking so much about Someday and start making This Day your focus. This Day might be busy. It might be full of distractions. It might hold unexpected problems or take unexpected turns. But This Day is also full of potential. This Day offers you an opportunity to make progress on whatever your life goal is. And This Day is here, right now. Someday may never come.

It's okay to think about and plan for Someday, but This Day is the one where you either gain ground or lose it.

If you are going to own the day, you have to own the hour, and you have to own the minute.

Aubrey Marcus

For Further Reflection

Luke 19:5; Matthew 6:34

TODAY'S PRAYER

Father, I know that every day is a gift,
an opportunity to serve you and to become
more of what you want me to be.
Give me a passion for This Day and
help me trust you with Someday.

Movement

I will guide you along the best pathway for your life.

PSALM 32:8

It's interesting how much of the advice we get (and give) has to do with remaining stationary.

~ Hold your horses.

~ Hang in there.

~ Settle down.

~ Stand pat.

~ Stay put.

~ Relax.

One would almost think the secret to a great life is to dig in your heels. But thousands of verses in the Bible communicate the importance of motion in regard to a healthy relationship with God. We're told to *walk* with God, to *run* the race, to *follow* Jesus, to *go* into all the world. Honestly, a person could get worn out just reading all those verses that command us to be on the move.

It's important to understand that as you grow stronger and healthier in your spiritual life, you must not stop. Even after this devotional journey is complete, you must find a way to keep the momentum going. Stick with your daily devotions, surround yourself with positive people who will encourage you and not judge you, and get involved in Christian service if you aren't already. You will have come a long way, but you won't be where you need to be. You will actually never be where you need to be this side of heaven, but you can always be moving in the right direction. That's really the goal—not perfection, but movement in the right direction.

Futurecasting is all about movement. Being able to get started and then build and maintain momentum is critical to the entire process.

Brian David Johnson

For Further Reflection

James 1:22; 1 Timothy 4:15

TODAY'S PRAYER

Father in heaven, on those days when I feel like quitting, encourage me to keep moving. And if I refuse, push me.

Tell Yourself the Truth

You will know the truth,
and the truth will set you free.

JOHN 8:32

Lying is one of the most common sins. Surveys indicate that the average adult cannot have a 10-minute conversation without lying at least once. If you're wondering who gets lied to the most, it's parents. And if you're wondering where the largest percentage of false statements are made, it's dating sites.

One issue the research doesn't address is people lying to themselves. Perhaps this is the biggest problem of all. Maybe the sin you committed that brought shame into your life was the result of lies you told yourself, such as:

- "I'm clever enough to keep this a secret."

- "I'm strong enough not to go too far."

- "I can't live without him/her."

- "I can quit anytime I want."

- "I can't help it."

If you want to get spiritually healthy again and stay that way, tell yourself the truth. Here's a suggestion: Ask a close friend to hold you accountable when you say something that sounds like an excuse, a rationalization, or an inaccurate assessment of reality. This person should be someone who loves you enough and has a strong enough personality to challenge you and argue with you if need be. You won't like it when it happens, but those conversations might be what keeps you from doing an about-face and heading back into trouble. The truth, even if it hurts, will go a long way toward keeping you free.

I'm not a fan of positive thinking. Positive thinking says you can have the third piece of cheesecake and it won't hurt you. I am a fan of accurate thinking.

Daniel G. Amen

For Further Reflection

Psalm 86:11; Psalm 145:18

TODAY'S PRAYER

Lord Jesus, as the Way, the Truth,
and the Life, I know you abhor lies.
Help me to abhor them too, even when they
offer me an easier path temporarily.

More Than Sorry

*Put to death the sinful, earthly things
lurking within you.*

COLOSSIANS 3:5

When you were a child, your parents probably taught you to say you were sorry when you did something wrong. But did you always say it sincerely? Maybe you got into a scuffle with a sibling and left him or her crying. Your mom demanded that you apologize, which you did. And then when she left the room, you popped your sibling again for getting you in trouble.

The word *sorry* is important—but it needs to be uttered sincerely. How many times have you seen a politician or celebrity issue an apology for some questionable behavior, only to think afterward that the person didn't really sound all that sorry? How many times did the apology itself sound like it was written by a PR person instead?

You might need to apologize to people because of the sin you committed. If so, do it. But expect them to be skeptical. An apology is not going to fix everything. It's needed, but it's not a magic word. You must be more than sorry—you need to show changed behavior that proves that what you say is more than a strategic PR move.

Say you're sorry and then back it up by actions that demonstrate how you *really* feel about what you did.

There is a big difference between being sorry and being changed.

Lysa TerKeurst

For Further Reflection

Revelation 2:5; Psalm 43:14

TODAY'S PRAYER

Dear Father, I know words are important.
Give me the wisdom to say the right ones.
But help me not to stop with words. Show me
also what I need to do to prove I am changed.

Antisocial Media

Examine yourselves to see if your faith is genuine.

2 CORINTHIANS 13:5

According to the Pew Research Center, about 69 percent of adults and 81 percent of teenagers use social media. This statistic becomes frightening when you consider the problems social media can cause in people's lives, such as anxiety, depression, envy, jealousy, and what some are calling FOMO—the fear of missing out. Social media platforms are also places where lies and propaganda flourish and bullying occurs. There have now been many instances where people have committed suicide because of interactions they had on social media.

As a person who is trying to bounce back from some bad choices and overcome shame, you should seriously weigh whether social media is a net positive or negative in your life. Going forward, you're going to need a positive attitude and outlook. You're going to need to focus on your own issues and not get caught up in other people's drama. Most of all, you're going to need to be thinking about the things of heaven, not the things of earth.

The good news? More and more people are getting off social media and reporting that they are much happier and have less stress and more time. They get things done more quickly and efficiently because they aren't constantly checking their phones. Their relationships are benefiting as well because they talk face to face and make eye contact instead of using text-speak and emojis.

Think about it. Pray about it. Getting off social media might really help you.

We spend more time studying and questioning the lives and motivations of others on Facebook then we do studying and questioning our own lives and motivations.

Kasey Van Norman

For Further Reflection

2 Peter 3:11; Matthew 6:6

TODAY'S PRAYER

Lord Jesus, forgive me for all the times I have shown more interest in a Twitter thread than in your Word. Help me to master social media instead of allowing it to master me.

Driver's Seat Theology

*So humble yourselves under
the mighty power of God.*

1 PETER 5:6

If you walk into a Christian bookstore, you'll likely find an abundance of trinkets—T-shirts, coffee mugs, key chains, bookmarks, ball caps, bracelets, and bumper stickers— competing with the latest bestsellers for shelf space. Two bumper sticker slogans in particular have been wildly popular through the years. One encourages, "Honk if you love Jesus." The other says, "God is my co-pilot."

Do you think God is troubled by that second phrase? Wouldn't he expect to be the pilot and for us to be the co-pilots?

If you reflect on the trouble you've had, the sin you committed that brought you shame, you'll realize you put yourself in the pilot's seat, and God wasn't on the plane at all. If you want to move forward and not repeat your sin, this mindset and behavior must change. You have to set aside your own desires and commit to doing what God wants.

Many people—perhaps most people—struggle with surrendering their wills because they're afraid if God pilots their lives, he won't go where they want to go. He might not. But he will go where they *need* to go. One of the great secrets of a happy Christian life is to make sure you're sitting in the proper seat when your life takes off.

So many times I've shaken my fist at God and told him that if he'd just listen to me, he'd see that my plan is really, really good.

Emily Ley

For Further Reflection

Psalm 115:3; Job 42:2

TODAY'S PRAYER

Lord, I tend to want to run my life my way. Help me to remember the disaster I created the last time I did, and to appreciate the wisdom of simply humbling myself under your authority.

The Bad Thing About Being Good

Guard your heart above all else,
for it determines the course of your life.

PROVERBS 4:23

Remember when you were a kid and your parents left you with a sitter? What was the last thing your mom said to you as she walked out the door? It was probably, "Be good!"

Every parent has said this to their child. We don't want our kids to embarrass us, and we certainly don't want to get a call from the babysitter that necessitates us coming home early.

From an early age we're told to behave. And being good is, well, good. However, there's one situation when trying to be good is a bad idea. It's that moment when we decide it's the answer to our messed-up lives: "If I just stop doing that, I'll be OK."

In Proverbs 4:23, God says the course (or the direction, the quality) of our lives will be determined not by our behavior, but by our hearts. Our hearts direct our choices, our choices determine our behavior, and our behavior produces a life that either pleases or displeases God. If you really want to correct your life and keep it on track, focus on your heart. Your behavior will take care of itself if your heart is right.

Trying to be good without a clean heart won't work. It's like putting a new paint job on a car that has a bad engine.

Fix the engine first, and then the paint job will actually mean something.

Broken character isn't repaired by new behavior; it's repaired by new beliefs.

Nona Jones

For Further Reflection

1 Samuel 16:7; Proverbs 27:19

TODAY'S PRAYER

Father, create in me a clean heart. Look inside me and reveal those areas that need attention. And help me as I work to make corrections.

The Tongue

No human being can tame the tongue.
It is restless and evil, full of deadly poison.

JAMES 3:8

We live in an age of words. Researchers have been working around the clock to find an American over the age of 20 who doesn't have a blog or a podcast, but so far they have come up empty. I'm joking, of course. But doesn't it seem like everyone has a platform from which they promote their ideas? One young pastor recently said, "I don't really want to start a podcast, but I almost feel like I have to because all my friends are doing it, and they think I'm slacking."

Proverbs 10:19 says, "Too much talk leads to sin. Be sensible and keep your mouth shut." What kind of sin is he talking about? Probably any sin of the tongue. If you can't keep your mouth shut, you'll probably end up gossiping, betraying a confidence, boasting, exaggerating, harshly criticizing someone, or saying something misleading in an effort to benefit yourself.

Your words can make or break you—and others. Many people today are wounded and broken because of things that have been said to them. Maybe the sin that has brought you shame is tied in some way to things that were said to you. Were you lied to? Seduced? Given false hope?

As you seek to build a better life, you will be wise to talk less. You don't have to always state your opinion or participate in every conversation. And you don't have to post on social media, which sometimes only serves to instigate drama, provoke people, or make you—or someone else—appear foolish. Speak when you have something worth saying; otherwise, keep quiet.

If I had it all to do over again, I'd study more and preach less.

Billy Graham

For Further Reflection

James 1:26; Proverbs 18:21

TODAY'S PRAYER

Dear heavenly Father, help me to care
more about your words than my own.
Give me the wisdom to know when
to speak and when to keep silent.

Don't Try Harder

*Only in returning to me and resting
in me will you be saved.*

Isaiah 30:15

You may have glanced at the title of today's devotion and thought it was a misprint. Isn't trying hard the key to success? When you're watching a sporting event, don't the announcers often praise the team putting forth the most effort? When a game ends, don't the talking heads often say the winning players "wanted it more," meaning that their greater passion and effort carried them to victory?

Persistence is good. But putting in 100% effort is only beneficial if you're doing the right thing. A baseball player, for example, might put everything he has into a throw, but if he's throwing to the wrong base, that effort is wasted. A salesman might work 60 hours a week trying to increase his income, but if he doesn't deliver a good presentation, those hours produced little reward. Trying harder isn't always the answer.

The real secret of success is focusing on the right priorities. There are some things that are good and fun to do but aren't what we need to do first. Or we may be continually using the same approach on an old problem when really, a whole *new* approach needed to be developed.

As you look ahead, think, pray, or journal about what should take precedence in your life that will allow you to achieve your goals. Striving is good, but ordering your priorities so that God and your spiritual health come first will make the difference in whether or not your hard work pays off.

You really thought that if you gritted your teeth it would help you become a hero? Well, there's more to life than just gritting your teeth.

Linus, to Charlie Brown

For Further Reflection

Ecclesiastes 2:11; Ecclesiastes 2:22–23

TODAY'S PRAYER

Lord, help me understand the folly of constantly trying to do more. Instead, show me the right things on which to focus my energy so that my efforts won't go to waste.

The Power of Place

*When you pray, go away by yourself,
shut the door behind you,
and pray to your Father in private.*

MATTHEW 6:6

I know you think a lot about *what* you do, but do you ever think about where you do it? You might be surprised to know that Scripture often stresses *where* things happen.

For example, the Gospel writers specify that when Jesus prayed, he often found a place away from distractions. Peter's location when he betrayed Jesus is also emphasized because it had a lot to do with the fear that caused him to lie and claim that he didn't know Jesus. And what about where Jesus was born? God wanted us to know that it wasn't in a palace, but a stable. And then there are Paul's letters. It informs our understanding of them to know that some were written in prison. I could go on, but you get the idea. Places are important.

Think about the places of your life: where you live, work, play, and worship. Not every place is going to be a happy place, obviously. Your workplace, for example, might be a busy, high-stress environment. Your home might have tension in it. Even your church might be facing challenges right now. That's why, in our verse for today, Jesus stresses the importance of finding a peaceful, quiet place to spend time with him.

Do you have such a place?

If you don't, find one. Or make one.

You'll discover that your prayer life will be much more meaningful and easier to maintain if you can meet with God one-on-one with no distractions.

There is abundance of hearing, reading, talking, professing, visiting, contributing to the poor and teaching at schools. But is there, together with all this, a due proportion of private prayer?

J. C. Ryle

For Further Reflection
Luke 6:12; Luke 22:39

TODAY'S PRAYER

Father, help me to see the importance
of spending time alone with you.
May I never fail to seek out those quiet
times with you the way Jesus did.

Be Smart

*For the LORD grants wisdom! From his mouth
come knowledge and understanding.*

PROVERBS 2:6

It's incredible how many "smart" products are on the market. There are smart phones, TVs, cars, security systems, doorbells, baby monitors, thermostats, light bulbs, toasters, coffee makers, vacuums, grills, and exercise bikes to name a few. They're designed to make life easier, and in some ways they do. But some people with a house full of smart products still lead miserable lives. They're still stressed out, worried, lonely, frustrated, arguing with their kids, and filing for divorce.

What we need is not to buy more smart products, but to make smarter choices.

There's a very good chance that the sin you committed that brought you shame was, to put it bluntly, really dumb. Maybe you reflected on it after the fact and wondered how you could have been so stupid. You wouldn't be the first.

Think about what drives your decision-making. Do you have a friend or relative you listen to? Are you a fan of podcasts or media self-help gurus such as Dr. Phil? Do you have a shelf full of books you've bought that focus on the issues you struggle with? It's not that these things offer no help at all, it's just that there's a much better place to go for help in making important life decisions: the Word of God.

Some people call it the Good Book. We could call it the Smart Book.

Imagine, your Creator has written a life instruction book just for you. And you're going to read Dr. Phil instead? Really?

Do yourself a favor and let the Smart Book be your guide.

God calls us to obey him not simply because it's right but because it's smart. He warns us against disobedience not just because it's wrong but also because it's stupid.

Randy Alcorn

For Further Reflection

Proverbs 18:15; Proverbs 16:16

TODAY'S PRAYER

Dear Father, I am embarrassed by the stupidity of some of my choices. Forgive me for not turning to your Word first, and help me never to make that mistake again.

Be Real

Not everyone who calls out to me, 'Lord! Lord!'
will enter the Kingdom of Heaven.

MATTHEW 7:21

When people make big mistakes that result in the collapse of their families, careers, or reputations, it's not unusual for them to start searching for God. There's no doubt that many of these people are sincere and really do find God. But some people turn to God the way sick people turn to a bottle of aspirin, out of desperation to find relief from their pain. Then, when some time passes and the pain goes away, God is no longer a priority.

Maybe you didn't come to this book as a Christian, but more out of desperation. Your life was a wreck and you felt terrible shame, so you were willing to try something—anything—that might help. Maybe you have friends who love God and have tried to witness to you. When things were sailing along just fine, you weren't interested, but when disaster came you thought, "What do I have to lose?"

This book would not be complete without a caution about the danger of merely using God rather than truly committing to him. There is no promise in the Bible, no blessing of God, that is guaranteed to people who see God as expendable— something to turn to when they're feeling pain but ignore the rest of the time. God is not looking for that kind of relationship with anybody. In fact, our verse for today is a stark reminder that God knows who's sincere in their faith and who's just using him.

Always remember that God never asks you to be perfect, but he does ask you to be real.

The danger of religion is it inspires people to claim their identities as "Christians" while they continue to think exactly like the rest of the world.

David and Jason Benham

For Further Reflection

1 John 3:18; Romans 12:9

TODAY'S PRAYER

Lord Jesus, your words in today's verse are a bit scary. Help me to live in such a way that I never have to worry about hypocrisy being my downfall.

Ready, Set, Grow!

*You must grow in the grace and knowledge
of our Lord and Savior Jesus Christ.*

2 PETER 3:18

Sometimes people confuse the end with the beginning.

A new mother, after a long and difficult pregnancy, might celebrate the healthy birth of her child and say, "Whew, I'm glad that's over!" when in fact, the real challenge is just beginning.

A man who has cheated on his wife, apologized, and begged her not to file for divorce might say, "I'm so glad we saved our marriage!" when in fact, the real job of reestablishing trust is just beginning.

Right now, as this book is running out of pages, you might be getting the feeling that the hard work is behind you. It isn't; it's ahead of you. Even if you have wrestled honestly with the ideas and challenges presented in these devotions and come to a place of peace and closeness with God, you aren't done. The challenge as you close this book and set it aside in a couple of days is to keep growing in your faith. It isn't that hard to grow your faith, but it does take some thought and effort. Here are three suggestions.

First, go to church. You need to hear the Word preached and you need the strength and encouragement that comes naturally when you lock arms with others.

Second, stay in the Word. A 25-minute sermon on Sunday isn't enough. You will have negative voices in your ear every day. You only hurt yourself when you limit God's voice to a few minutes a week.

And third, pray like crazy. Your life will go better and the likelihood of you repeating your past mistakes will be greatly reduced if you keep the lines of communication open between you and God.

I know some people who have been saved for twenty-five years, but they don't have twenty-five years of experience. They have one year of experience repeated twenty-five times.

Mark Batterson

For Further Reflection
1 Peter 2:2; Philippians 1:9

TODAY'S PRAYER

Dear Lord, I am thankful to you for bringing me this far, for forgiving me and setting me back on my feet. Now help me to focus on my future so that I may never repeat my past.

Testimony Time

Has the LORD redeemed you?
Then speak out!

PSALM 107:2

Have you ever wondered how many stories are in the Bible? People have found it hard to count them because they often run together and it's hard to tell when one ends and another begins. However, the folks at Good Soil, who provide resources and support for people who teach the Bible, estimate that there are between 600 and 800.

God knows there is power in a story.

What you need to understand is that there is power in *your* story.

If the last 100 days have led you to repentance, profound changes in your heart and mind, and ultimately to peace with yourself and God, your story—your testimony—is worth sharing. Someone out there is where you were and needs the encouragement and hope your testimony would give.

I would offer two pieces of advice.

First, show the proper reverence as you tell your story. Remember that your sin is not the point; God's love, grace, and forgiveness is the point. He should be the star of your story, not you.

And second, write your testimony out and practice sharing it. This might sound like busywork, but it isn't. Your testimony will only have power if you can share it in a compelling way. If you ramble or focus on irrelevant details while missing the important points, your testimony will be robbed of its power. Don't misuse the opportunities God gives you by not being ready.

Our testimonies are the sacred battle histories of what Christ has done and won.

Nika Maples

For Further Reflection

1 Peter 3:15; Mark 5:19

TODAY'S PRAYER

Father in heaven, I praise you for
your mercy and grace and peace.
You have been far better to me than I deserve.
Help me as I tell others of your greatness.

Looking Ahead

Good planning and hard work lead to prosperity.

PROVERBS 21:5

As you come to the end of this devotional, it's important to look ahead. You've had a chance to think through some serious issues related to your sin, your guilt, your forgiveness, and your relationship with God. It's my prayer that you have come to a place of peace, knowing that you are forgiven and that the road ahead holds tremendous possibilities. But in the end, the future will be what you make it. Here are four simple suggestions I hope you will consider.

First, let your sin go. If God has forgiven you, you've been granted total freedom. For you to continue to haul a load of guilt around is pointless.

Second, accept—without bitterness—the consequences of your sin that may be lingering. Unfortunately, some of sin's consequences last a lifetime. I hope that is not the case in your situation, but if it is, face them with dignity and let them be a cautionary reminder when you encounter temptation in the future.

Third, choose carefully who you listen to. Like it or not, your sin has branded you in some people's minds. To them, you may forever wear Hester Prynne's scarlet letter. There's not much you can do about that, but you can choose to spend your time with and around people who love you and have forgiven you.

Finally, remember that your past was what you made it, and your future will be too. And it will be made today. So make today a good day. Honor God with your choices. Find a worthwhile purpose and chase it for all you're worth!

The best way to predict the future is to create it.

Abraham Lincoln

For Further Reflection

Proverbs 24:27; Proverbs 16:3

TODAY'S PRAYER

Dear heavenly Father, as I close this book and look ahead, I thank you for forgiving me, and I ask you to help me in my desire to honor you with my life from this day forward.

DEVOTIONALS FROM
STEPHEN ARTERBURN

100 Days of Character Daily Devotional
ISBN: 9781628624953

100 Days of Prayer Daily Devotional
ISBN: 9781628624281

100 Days of Peace Daily Devotional
ISBN: 9781628624960

100 Days of Healing Daily Devotional
ISBN: 9781628624946

100 Days to Freedom from Fear and Anxiety
Daily Devotional
ISBN: 9781628629965

100 Days to Freedom from Depression
Daily Devotional
ISBN: 9781628629972

100 Days to Freedom from Anger
Daily Devotional
ISBN: 9781628629989

www.hendricksonrose.com